Eng. by John Sartain Phil^a

Yrs Very Truly
John C. Lowrie

THE HEBREW LAWGIVER.

BY

JOHN M. LOWRIE, D.D.,

AUTHOR OF "ESTHER AND HER TIMES," AND "ADAM AND HIS TIMES."

PASTOR OF THE FIRST PRESBYTERIAN CHURCH,

FORT WAYNE, INDIANA.

"The Lawgiver of the Jews, no common man."—LONGINUS.

VOL. I.

PHILADELPHIA:

PRESBYTERIAN BOARD OF PUBLICATION,

No. 821 CHESTNUT STREET.

STEREOTYPED BY WESTCOTT & THOMSON.

CONTENTS.

VOL. I.

CHAPTER XX.

CHAPTER XXI.

CHAPTER XXII.

CHAPTER XXIII.

CHAPTER XXIV.

CHAPTER XXV.

CHAPTER XXVI.

CHAPTER XXVII.

PREFACE.

Possibly the volumes now laid before the Christian public may be thought by some readers to come quite short of the promise which their name implies. But certainly the most intelligent readers will be least surprised at this. For the full discussion of the character, claims, teachings and influence of the Hebrew Lawgiver would require more volumes than the chapters we here present; indeed the writings called forth by the Pentateuch would make a library in number far exceeding the pages of this work; nor will these volumes be issued in vain, even though containing little that is new, if they serve to awaken in their readers an interest in Scriptural teachings.

Yet a certain completeness is to be reasonably expected in a new publication; and the more familiar the subject, the more easily may any important omission be noticed. Chiefly, it may be thought, that decided attention should here be paid to the more recent attacks made upon the authority of Moses and the historical claims of his writings. These volumes would indeed be sadly defective without the careful urging of serious and weighty considerations to vindicate the authenticity of the books of Moses, and his entire credibility, not simply as a historian, but as the lawgiver of the Hebrew people and a prophet of the Most High God. So we have given due care to maintain these points. But no formal refutation has been attempted of attacks upon Moses, which deserve the name rather of cavillings than of arguments. These chapters were almost wholly written before the publication of even the first book of Bishop Colenso. Doubtless his writings, eagerly published on this side of the ocean, have gained a wide circulation and done their share of mischief, principally because their author has been, and indeed still is, a prelate in the English established church. But in this brief preface we may give a few reasons for making no elaborate reply to his writings; and in so doing express some thoughts touching the long controversy in which his cavillings bear their transient part.

No serious Christian can feel, or should affect, indifference, in view of the prevalence of infidelity, or the various assaults it makes upon the authority of the sacred canon. Yet not only a calm confidence in the strength of the Christian evidences becomes the intelligent believer; but also a knowledge of the blustering assumptions which the adversaries of truth are not a little prone to make; and an acquaintance with the methods that best tend to establish the serious claims of the Bible. One inexperienced in the conflicts of truth against the ragings of human depravity, is prone to judge unwisely. The loud congratulations of unbelievers upon the accession of a prelate to their ranks, the fears of timid Christians, and the numerous replies made to his books, might lead such an one to think that now something had occurred more serious than the annals of ecclesiastical warfare had ever before known; that now indeed has come the grand crisis of the war. Yet as well may the raw recruit, who now has his first actual experience of the turmoil of conflict, affirm that no such battle was ever fought before; as well, at his first sight of an eclipse, may an astronomer be alarmed lest the sun's light has been blotted for ever out; as the humble Christian begin to tremble, when men talk boastingly, as if the foundations were indeed destroyed. Ps. xi. 3. In the history of the church, fierce attacks upon the evidences of revealed religion are no new thing: with the exultant shouts of her foes, her sons should by this time be familiar; we cannot look back to any period when the cause of piety won easy victories, because there were none to oppose it, with all the swellings of tumultuous passion; there have been times of far deeper gloom than the present in the relative positions of faith and unbelief; and understanding now, better than ever, the just estimate in which we should hold the numbers, the temper, the arguments, and the influence of our adversaries, the friends of religion may stand firm and calm in their faith, and should know this, that we have no better or more effective defence against all assaults than the fair presentation of the "things which are most surely believed among us." Let the truth be known, and it shall not fail of victories.

It is an old remark that the adversaries of Christianity, since certainly they are unprepared to give the world any positive or satisfactory teachings instead of those they would take from us, have the least possible cause for wishing to gain converts to their opinions; yet few are so eager as they to have men adopt their views. As if in doubt themselves of the truthfulness of their affirmations, they desire to gain the assent of other minds; as if aware that the books written in support of religion cannot be systematically answered, they content themselves with objections against particular things, and these repeated with a wearisome and stupid pertinacity; as if anxious to win proselytes upon any terms, they catch eagerly at the opportunity of dignifying their opinions with a celebrated name; and so they, who decry all authority, yet fortify their cavillings with every possible authority, and strive to make their cause less invidious by showing upon their side as large numbers of as high-sounding names as possible.* This description of what the adversaries of the sacred writings have been, is as true of what they are. To know how numerous and strenuous have been our foes in the past; what has been the prevailing temper of their hostility; what we may expect in the future; and what therefore are the chief dangers against which we should guard, may serve to confirm us in the idea that simply to maintain the truth is the church's best defence.

"These things were not done in a corner;" said an eloquent advocate of Christianity upon an important public occasion. And his words belong to every later, and indeed to every earlier period of the history of the church. No stolen march upon the world has given influence or power to teachings, whose well-known tendency is to awaken the human mind; whose pathway in long centuries is marked by conflicts of which the world could not be ignorant; and

* Dr. Johnson, Life of Sir Thomas Browne.

yet whose enemies are chiefly remembered, because their names are associated with the happy triumphs and the growing strength of the Christian evidences. Truth has had her angry foes ever since the unaccepted offering of the first-born of man; the long succession of her enemies may be traced in history almost as clearly as the succession of her friends; this includes the names of men whose learning and position, whose zeal and intellectual ability gave promise of success in their efforts to subvert the foundations of the church of God, had success been possible in such an enterprise; and it seems most unlikely indeed, that any new enemies should ever be able to effect what these numerous foes have done so little to accomplish. We may expect that the religious history of our race, like our social experience, should present problems substantially the same, though in untried and perplexing forms, to each generation. Yet we do not anticipate that darker days will come than our brethren have already known; that any new principles must be taught to our children beyond those we already profess; or that we or they have before us any fiercer conflicts than already have been "accomplished in our brethren."

That period, within the seventeenth and eighteenth centuries, during which the spread and power of Deism filled England especially, with gloom, may well be recalled to our minds for its profitable lessons. Because of its origin, spirit, and results; because also of the strength imparted to the evidences of Christianity by the stern conflicts forced upon the friends of truth, scarcely any portion of ecclesiastical history is better worthy of our careful study. It was indeed a period of religious decline. How dolorous seems the key-note of lamentation struck forth by the fingers of an eminent prelate, in the dark days, when Christianity seemed almost to exist by sufferance. "It has come, I know not how," says Bishop Butler, in the preface to his immortal "ANALOGY," "to be taken for granted, by many persons, that Christianity is not so much as a subject of inquiry; but that it is now, at length, discovered to be fictitious. And accordingly they treat it, as if, in the present age, this were an agreed point, among all people of discernment. . . . . IT IS NOT HOWEVER SO CLEAR A CASE THAT THERE IS NOTHING IN IT." Could so intelligent a writer have penned such a sentence, except in a time of deep darkness upon the land; except as infidelity had not only reached a large, but almost a dominant power over the intelligent and influential minds of England? Yet his words are in wide contrast with the defiant tones, in which Bishop Warburton, twenty years later, boldly told the free-thinkers that he was ready to meet them upon a fair field, having no love for their cause, no fear of the abilities they used in its support; careless of their praises; and even ready to glory in their censures.

It does not fall in with the design of this preface to sketch the history of that gloomy period. A chief purpose in making this mention of it, is to recall the cheering truth, that as the origin and the results of the infidel philosophy in these centuries was the abounding of irreligion, so the controversies then awakened stirred the sluggish church to a new and vigorous life; and thus turned out "rather unto the furtherance of the gospel." Unquestionably, on the one hand, the corruption of public morals upon the restoration of the profligate Charles II. to the English throne, was a chief source of these false principles. Just as certainly, upon the other hand, the fearful scenes that convulsed Europe, and that especially belonged to the French revolution at the close of the last century, were the legitimate offspring of the same philosophy. It is not an easy thing for us to comprehend how fierce were the controversies of those times. We are prone to magnify the fears that address our own hearts and the dangers our own eyes see; we cannot conceive the swelling heights of their tides of irreligion and skepticism. Yet as the retiring flood often leaves upon the shore the proofs of its might, in the huge drifts which no ordinary storm could move; so a few facts from the abundant records of that conflict between falsehood and truth, may illustrate the fierceness of the strife. Among the promoters of infidel sentiments, no name deserves mention, for priority in time or in ability, beyond that of Thomas Hobbes. Yet is he but an example to remind us of the activities awakened by writings such as his. "Against Hobbes, says Warburton, the whole church militant took up arms. The answers to the *Leviathan* would form a library."* The same may be said of every writer whose ability or notoriety seemed worthy of reply; and of many whose notoriety at the end of a century was due to the fact that they had been answered. Thirty-five answers were made to Collins within two years; thirty thousand copies of Woolston's discourses

* Sir James Mackintosh, View, &c.

were sold—an immense issue in those times—and sixty replies were made to them; while more than a hundred authors wrote in refutation of Tindal. Let these incidents suffice to show the earnestness with which the assaults of those times were met, on the part of the friends of truth.

Of the character of these discussions we need not speak; yet would it be unjust to the cause of religion to forget the distinct allegation that but little credit is due to the infidel writers of every age upon the score of sincere efforts to reach the truth in their discussions. Infidelity is of the heart rather than of the head. After giving a sketch of the prevailing sentiment among them an excellent writer remarks: "The sum of the whole is this: modern unbelievers are Deists in theory, Pagans in inclination, and Atheists in practice."* We need not affirm that a candid, or at least a sincere, rejecter of the sacred writings is an impossible character. But certainly the usual path to infidelity is not through the serious and earnest investigations that befit rational men; its usual tendencies are downward to all that degrades both public and private morals; and its usual characteristics are not such as to inspire any large degree of respect for its advocates. These charges have often been made before; the well-known words of Rousseau may prove them, though he is as liable himself to similar censures; and they are as palpably true before the eyes of the world as they ever have been. Bishop Colenso exhibits no new phase of infidel ethics, when he openly attacks the foundations of Christi-

* A. Fuller's Works, i. 111.

anity, yet persistently professing his attachment to the church, holding his place among the prelates of the establishment, and receiving the honours and emoluments that pertain to this office.

It may be said, that the controversy between faith and unbelief is one of grand principles: that peculiarities of personal character and conduct have but little to do in settling it; and that dangerous opinions owe their importance chiefly to the interests they put in jeopardy. But on the one hand, we are unwilling to allow that the manifest tendency of certain principles must be laid aside from our thoughts, when the very thing in controversy involves the highest morality; and on the other hand, the character of our opponents usually determines how the discussion of our differences may be best conducted. The advocates of Christianity have not shrunk back, in other days, nor in our own, from the closest encounters with error. And not a few good results have sprung from the struggles of the past. We have said that the evidences of Christianity received large support from the conflicts of the seventeenth and eighteenth centuries; we may add that better views have succeeded the extreme literary skepticism that prevailed a few years ago in Germany; and we have recently read that the Life of Jesus by M. Renan has induced many European Jews to read the true history, as given in the Gospels, through their desire to compare the teachings of the New Testament with the misrepresentations of the French professor. We would fairly meet every opposer; and yet there are ways of upholding the truth though we say little against the cavillings of foes, whom we cannot respect.

We have said that fairly to present the truth is a most effective defence against the assaults of error. There are many reasons for this. We mean no comparison between the external and the internal evidences of Christianity. We affirm that all the genuine arguments to support the truth are in harmony; and that no advocate of Christianity is at liberty to make light of any evidences to maintain it. Yet circumstances must govern the wise presentation of the truth, either to convince or persuade: and he may be faithful whose teachings are far from complete. Let the errorist be directly attacked; let the ignorant be carefully instructed; let the serious Christian make himself acquainted, as fully as possible, with the reasons for our hopes, and, in the best sense, be ever ready to answer every gainsayer. 1 Pet. iii. 15. But the present aspects of skepticism demand that we should place the careful exhibition of truth itself among our prominent means of disseminating truth, and allow the living word to be its own defence. Let men know what the Scriptures teach. They who will not read such writings may not be expected to read upon Christian evidences; and those who wish truly to understand the reasons of our faith can find no better than the faith itself affords.

We especially mean to say that in the changing aspects of infidelity, the latest form of skepticism demands that we should exhibit, more clearly than ever, the glorious system of revealed truth. Infidelity now feels the want of warm and life-giving principles that shall satisfy the religious cravings of the heart. We do not question that the knowledge of Christian truth quickens these irrepressible aspirations; as we are very certain that the Bible alone can satisfy them. Divine truth is like light: "it reveals itself and other things;" it shines indirectly where it does not shine directly; the clear statement of truth is an argument for the truth; and the friends of religion have ever claimed that a self-evidencing power belongs to the word of God. It is impossible that men should have even an imperfect knowledge of true religion without the quickening of the conscience: and it is impossible that the conscience should be truly satisfied but through the teachings God has revealed for that end. Infidelity in our age has been forced to the confession that man has religious wants; and to an intelligent mind nothing seems more lamentable than the strenuous efforts which skeptics make to persuade themselves and their disciples that religion would lose nothing in the overthrow of Christianity. In this state of things the truth has everything to gain by the fair presentation, less of the grounds of our faith, than of our faith itself. Let men know what the Bible teaches, and they will be more than prepared to detect the untruthfulness of the infidel arguments. They can indeed see the refutations of infidelity in its very statements; for when M. Renan says, that Jesus did not intend to work miracles but assumed to do so to gratify the demands of the age, and yet makes him "the incomparable man to whom the universal conscience defers as a teacher," he but betrays the unavoidable inconsistency of all who do not receive and acknowledge the entire claims of the PRE-EMINENT ONE. But they who truly know the Scriptures can do more than detect inconsistencies and false reasonings. They are ready to compare true religion with its shadow; the living, breathing form, with the cold misshapen manikin. Infidelity is not a system, and can never be fashioned into any agreement with itself. Not only are its affirmations capricious and arbitrary as any reveries of a disordered imagination, its teachings changeful and contradictory, its promises vague in expression and deceitful in performance, and its advocates not even respectful to each other; but it has nothing to meet the deep necessities of the human soul. A poor, dying woman, was lately surrounded by the miserable counsellors, whose teachings had led her to their hopeless creed, and in her latest unhappy moments was exhorted by them to hold on. "I am willing to hold on," said she, "if you will only tell me what I must hold to!"

Let the consistent teachings of the Bible, a grand system of truth, whose efficacy has been known for ages, be set before the minds of men; and it will commend itself "to every man's conscience in the sight of God." As "they that are whole need not a physician," men may neglect these teachings in their hours of pride: yet thousands of men can never be infidels in view of what they know of Christianity; and in times of change, sorrow, and seriousness, the heart will crave the consolations which only Divine revealings can afford. Not only is there a simplicity in all the Scriptural teachings well adapted to secure confidence in them—as the mien of a witness has as much to do with our confidence in him as his words; but there is an adaptation in these truths to awaken and to satisfy the souls of men, that can never pertain to falsehood. And it is the more important to make these teachings known, because every man in our communities has personal acquaintances, whose characters he is compelled to respect, and whose professions, comforts, activities and hopes are intelligible only when he also knows the holy principles from which they spring. We cannot separate faith and unbelief from their manifest fruits around us. We are content to abide by this test.

Here we may interpose a few words concerning the scientific infidelity of modern days. We can understand how an ardent mind, enlisted in the zealous pursuit of truth, having but a small acquaintance with the vast evidences that support the Christian system, and filled with prejudices because the claims of science are sometimes denied, might be arrayed in opposition to the Scriptures: though we cannot allow that any wise man can esteem the reconciliation of religion and science as a trivial matter; nor count him a good man who is indifferent to the high claims of the Bible. It could scarcely be otherwise than that science and religion in our times should have their apparent conflicts; new questions must spring up when the wonderful discoveries of our age are compared with teachings, the latest of which are eighteen centuries old: for the exact reconciliation of matters which at first are but half understood on either side, no man was prepared; and the chief thing needful for all concerned is to possess a patient, truth-loving spirit. Doubtless much strife has arisen here from a double ignorance, *first* of what the Scriptures really affirm; and *next* of what true science affirms; as we compare the exact truth of both with what their respective votaries, have said on their behalf. The friends of the Bible, while refusing what it has been thought to teach, may abide by its true teachings. Christians have been mistaken in their understanding of the Scriptures; scientific men have made serious mistakes touching science; and both have been at times misrepresented.* We feel confident that all the apparent issues between the Bible and science can be settled, when both are fairly understood; because, we doubt not, God is the Author of both. Here is room for serious, candid discussion; and earnest men should be met in this spirit. Let not the friends of religion be timid at the investigations and progress of science; let not the devotees of science exult at the seeming overthrow of religion. The result will show that both are in the wrong: and in looking forward to the full adjustment of all these questions, "he that believeth shall not make haste."

We are free to confess that we fear infidelity; all its cavillings, and especially the seasons of its abounding. Yet not because of its superior arguments, or of the danger of its ultimate prevalence over religion. We fear it,

* It seems singular that so many writers should copy the charge of Dr. Hitchcock, (Religion and Geology, p. 11,) against Francis Turrettine, an eminent theologian of the sixteenth century, that he maintained with nice logic, the revolution of the sun around the earth. No such thesis can be found in his works. It appears in a compend of Turrettine, which was partly taken from the works of Leonardo Ryssenius, and not published till after the death of Turrettine himself. Doubtless this was the opinion of his time; but he should be held responsible only for his own writings. The compend adds other topics, not in Turrettine's works.

just as we do a pestilence or a contagious disease. For these we may have physicians and remedies; yet may they prove fatal to many of our children or our neighbours, in spite of all sanitary precautions. Infidelity ruins the souls of men; this is cause enough to dread its power even over one person. But that it springs from human depravity, that it addresses the fallen heart of man, and that its power is increased by its downward tendencies—as it is ever easier to destroy than to build up—may make us fear it more. And these very considerations give sufficient proofs that our conflicts with infidelity, as they have lasted all the life-time of the church, so cannot be confined to any place or time, but shall be continued as long as the earthly church stands.

There may be strange changes hereafter, as there have been, in the attitudes of the assaulting forces. The very arguments, by which Celsus would have overthrown Christianity, are now conceded as among the prime elements demanded in proof of its Divine origin; for indeed the gospel has created a public sentiment in Christendom, which its enemies would fain ascribe to the teachings of nature. In the eyes of the Pagan philosopher,* no mean judge of what man can know without revelation, a gospel preached to the poor and proposing to bring the race to receive the same religious teachings, was the very height of absurdity! Yet infidelity is ready now to concede that the gospel should be irrespective of persons, and that a God who is not for all the earth is for none of it. So Celsus acknowledged the historical verity of the Christian

* Neander's Church History, i. 90.

miracles, but maintained that they proved nothing; while modern infidelity, despairing of all efforts to invalidate this proof by historical deductions, and unable to deny the just inferences from it, if admitted, contents itself with a metaphysical sophistry that denies the possibility of miracles. But whatever changes may occur, let us not expect the overthrow of skepticism. We often hear the assertion that the battle of Christian evidences is to be fought out on *this* or *that* field. Let no man dream of this. Defeated, our enemies often will be, as they have been. But the church begins a new strife with each new age of men. As it is impossible so to convert any generation that we shall not need to preach repentance to their successors; as every man needs regeneration, no matter what may have been the faith of his fathers; so this battle is with human depravity; and it is not to be expected that we shall see the end of the strife, until men no longer inherit the fallen nature of our unhappy family.

This however is our comfort, that infidel activities, even aggressions, do not prove the decline of the church of God. Usually they precede or attend unusual activities among believing men. Some of the most glorious revivals of piety have been preceded by prevailing skepticism. The corruptions of the apostate church gave origin to much of this, which rapidly disappeared before the powerful preaching of the Reformers; in the midst of the English Deism began that great revival in which Whitefield and the Wesleys bore so large a part: the missionary enterprises of these modern times took their rise in the very height of the French revolution; some of the most remarkable awakenings of the western continent have taken place in times of deep depression; and the church often calls forth hostilities by the very zeal that maintains her own life. Infidelity has often been the pioneer of religion; has abounded when religion was advancing; and often gives token of the activities of the church.

We acknowledge the high importance of controversial writings wisely prepared. But because no particular phase of infidelity holds long dominion over the minds of men; because persons, already skeptically inclined, seldom care to hear calm discussions or to read religious books; because also of the thoughts already suggested, we reach this conclusion; that the best antidote for infidelity is the careful instruction of our families in the simple teachings of God's word. A mind well acquainted with what the Bible really says, is fortified against the cavillings of error. The objections of Colenso and Renan betray a carping temper that must disgust an intelligent and serious student: they are founded upon misconceptions that would not have occurred to men fit to teach others: it is hard to consent that they are candidly uttered.

These pages are designed to make their readers better acquainted with Moses and his inspired teachings. So doing, they will vindicate his claims to our confidence. Yet objections may be made, which even a well taught disciple cannot answer; all this without disturbing in the least his well grounded faith. The truth of religion—as Bishop Butler forcibly remarks—is to be judged of, by the force of all the arguments taken together. And we may add, that yet more unanswerable objections wait upon the denial of it! Beyond question we have no means to use for establishing the authority of the sacred writings at all to be compared with the teachings which make us better understand the Scriptures themselves. A knowledge of the Bible is the Bible's strong defence; an intelligent mind joined to a loving heart can make these defences impregnable.

THE HEBREW LAWGIVER.

CHAPTER I.

MOSES AND HIS BIOGRAPHY.

"Part not with these old names, each one of which
Bears in its bosom precious histories,
The life-deeds and death-conflicts of the men
From out whose loins we spring, the men of might
And wisdom, who have won such victories
Of truth for us." BONAR.

PROFITABLE teachings must ever awaken deep interest in the minds they address. A connected train of events is well adapted to secure the attention, and we acquire knowledge with the most ease and pleasure when it is associated with historical or personal narration. And doubtless the greatest degree of interest is secured when the history refers to one particular object: when the single object is presented to us like a vast painting from the hand of a skilful artist. A great historical or imaginative painting may be crowded with various figures; we may study each person and thing separately; we may read individual character and the ruling thought of the time in each face; we could not regard it as an interesting painting if we saw manifest blemishes, even in the minor figures or expressions; and yet, as a painting, it must express one thought from the artist's mind: usually there is one chief figure occupying the foreground, drawing the principal attention to itself, and giving character to the whole from the interest that attaches to this chief thing. The most exquisite finish of the separate parts, without a definite object in the whole, could not secure our interest, or give us the highest pleasure. Yet things in themselves incongruous, or even unsightly, may be grouped together with pleasing effect, if we can see the intelligent design of the mind that placed them there. In Hogarth's last painting, "The End of all things," there is an ingenious collection of objects that have no possible bond of connection, except just what the great artist wished to signify.*

It is because our interest thus easily gathers around a particular and definite object, that a universal history is less interesting than the history of some particular nation; that in reading a national history, we feel specially interested in the scenes of some eventful period, or the exploits of some particular hero; and that the biographies of eminent men are ever read with interest. Fictitious writings—such as novels and dramas—derive their popularity from the bold relief in which they hold forth a special person; and the more

* Lossing's Hist. Fine Arts, 251.

the readers can be made to sympathize with this principal personage, the greater is the success of the volume. Deprive such writings of the central figure; make the scenes in which he acts totally unlikely and unnatural; prevent the reader from sympathizing with the hero, and he is easily disgusted with the story. But unhappily, both in the writers and readers of fiction, morbid tastes are too easily acquired; the mind may be trained to love the romantic; and real life, and life's most important duties are made tasteless by books that have nothing in them of value and interest except as they gratify a diseased imagination.

Except for those who have spoiled the mind's healthful appetite by the dissipation of romance-reading, every superiority belongs to those truthful teachings which bring before us a real character, and give us a truthful delineation of the events of his life. Truth is at once the pleasure and the food of the soul. When we read fact, not fancy, truths, not tales, we need not dismiss the thoughts as soon as they pass through the mind; but we may live upon them, and we grow by them. And as some times are more worthy than others of the historian's pen: because their incidents are of more intrinsic interest, because they teach us more important lessons, and because they have exerted a larger influence upon subsequent history: so some men stand forth in past generations great in character, great in deeds, great in principles recorded upon enduring pages, great in influence upon their own and later times; and thus worthy of reverence in all succeeding generations.

Few names in the history of the past are worthy of more respect; few lives possess a more romantic interest; few times have been so critical, or have exerted a larger influence upon later ages, than the name, and life, and times of the great Lawgiver of the Jewish people.

The intellectual capacity of this most remarkable man we can learn not only from the great things he accomplished for his people, but also from his writings, the most ancient and the most remarkable which the world possesses. His high and disinterested patriotism is manifest, from the noble hour when he threw from his own neck the golden yoke he might have worn, perhaps even upon the Egyptian throne, until he broke the iron bondage that held his race in slavery, and led them towards the land so long promised to them in the covenant of God. We may see his love for his people in a hundred lessons of forbearance with their perverseness; of pleadings for their forgiveness with an offended God; and of steadfast refusal ever to secure a private end at the cost of public duty. His eminent piety began with the cheerful renunciation of Egyptian pleasures and prospects; was maintained by a holy intercourse such as man never before held face to face with God; and calls us yet to gratitude for the assurance that the Divine condescension ever stoops so low to meet the longings of the human heart. His life, beyond that of any other man, abounds in great scenes. Born at an eventful time, preserved and educated in a remarkable manner, and spending the very prime of his years in engagements of which we know nothing, and which were of insignificant importance, except as they formed his training for affairs of the greatest moment; at an age when most men have finished their work and look forward to the grave, he entered upon the period of his active life. Forty years were passed in wondrous doings. And at the end of this time, his death alone in the presence of his God; his burial by the hands of his Maker; and the concealment of his resting-place from the knowledge of mortals, may be regarded as the fitting close of so strange a history. Surely it is not for lack of interesting incidents if our attention is not awakened, as we attempt to contemplate the Life of the Jewish Lawgiver.

There is a sense in which we may regard Moses as the FOUNDER of the JEWISH NATION. It was not indeed until after his time that they had any land they could call their own; even during the bondage in Egypt, they had their elders, and principles and laws to bind them together; but they had never lived separate from other nations until he led them forth into the desert; their numbers had before been too insignificant to rank them in the class of nations; and a formal national government was secured to them at the foot of Sinai. Four hundred years had more than passed since God had called Abram forth from Ur of the Chaldees; had chosen him for his friend, Jas. ii. 23; and had given him promises of blessings in days to come. These promises included the fulfilment through Abraham of more ancient promises already given to the church of God. Especially they included the descent through Abraham of the Seed of the Woman, predicted in the earliest revelation after the fall of man, Gen. iii. 15. Gal. iii. 16. This prophecy was already the rallying point of hope, and faith, and joy, around which believers of every age had gathered: and it was only to call forth higher faith and expectations until the great day when its fulfilment would unfold the fulness of its meaning. The increase and preservation of his family, and to this end the possession of the land of Canaan, were means subsidiary to the completion of the promise in Messiah's coming and the heirship of the world. Rom. iv. 13.

We need not marvel, if the eye of the strongest faith could scarcely look forward through so many centuries of change and darkness; if the Jewish fathers put a carnal and insufficient interpretation upon the promises to Abraham; and if even yet, to the superficial observer, the Jewish church seemed vested with privileges and honoured with powers exclusively for themselves, and not as temporary trustees, preserving oracles, and principles, and promises, to bless all the nations of the earth. But let us not adopt a theory so inadequate to solve the questions which gather around these great promises of God: so far short of the clear explanations of Paul the Apostle—a name not less to be held in honour in the church of God than that of Moses.

THE BLESSED PROMISE first spoken in the ears of Adam, renewed in solemn covenant with Abraham, the great burden of all the old Testament teachings, could not find its fulfilment in that economy, nor within the narrow confines of Judea. It did not give the HEIR himself until the Messiah came, Gal. iii. 16: the covenant made of God with Abraham, promising that in HIS SEED all nations of the earth should be blessed, Gen. xii. 3, xvii. 5, Gal. iii. 8, did not begin its greatest triumphs till the subsequent and subordinate covenant, made with Moses at Sinai, was ready to pass away, Gal. iii. 17–19, Heb. viii.: ever since the fall of the Jewish temple and the abrogation of the Levitical dispensation, the blessing of Abraham comes on the Gentiles, and they receive the Holy Spirit; Gal. iii. 14; and all the triumphs of the gospel of Christ yet in the future, are part of the blessing promised to all the nations of the earth through the friend of God.

But if Paul can truly say that all these believers of the Old Economy received not the promise, because God gives us the better things to which they but looked forward, Heb. xi. 39, 40, we may also reckon that a new era of Jewish history begins with Moses. With him begins the distinctive national existence. To Abraham, Isaac, and Jacob, God gave in Canaan not a footbreadth of inheritance, Acts vii. 5. Even if we suppose that Abraham was already the head of a tribe when he came from Ur; that the "three hundred and eighteen" men capable of bearing arms spoken of in one place, Gen. xiv. 14, were retainers or vassals;* that these continued their allegiance to his sons; and without any express mention, passed down with Jacob into Egypt, still they were rather a tribe than a nation. When, in Egypt, the rule of a single patriarch was exchanged for that of twelve, and the people increased greatly in number, these things were in preparation for their further history.

Moses was their first Lawgiver. The constitution adopted at Sinai gave them first an existence truly national. Interpreting the whole by the subsequent results, and by the teachings of the New Testament, we may see the Divine design. Moses and his Institutions were intermediate between Abraham and Christ: not abrogating the covenant of the former, but passing away at the promised coming of the latter. The Levitical institutions embodied principles of eternal truth that could neither wax old nor pass away, Heb. xii. 27; but their national form and their ceremonial observ-

* Princeton Review, 1860, 13.

ances were to last from the setting up of the tabernacle in the wilderness only until the types should be answered in the coming of Him to whom they all gave witness. In short, the Jewish national existence, like the law of Moses, was to last till the SEED should come to whom the promise was made. So Jacob predicted on his dying bed, Gen. xlix. 10. So Paul interprets the Covenant made with Abraham. And the setting up of the Christian church; and the manifest dealings of God's providence which has scattered the Jews abroad in all the earth from that time until this, without a ruler or a priest, a sacrifice or a temple, prove the Divine Purpose. The national existence of Israel under the institutions of their first lawgiver, was to be lost when the Shiloh, the Messiah came.

Moses is the great character of the Jewish church. Yet WE have no ordinary interest in him; for he belongs to us almost as truly as to them. The faith of Moses is substantially our faith. The Books of Moses are our inspired instructors. The Moral Law given by his instrumentality on Sinai yet remains, the perfect rule for our direction—unrivalled in the felicitous expression of all that man should do; sanctioned in all its authority by every succeeding prophet, and by the Son of God himself. Even the ritual of Moses has not so passed away but that we may discern the precious foreshadowings of the gospel of Christ in its mysterious services and costly offerings. Moses stands before us far more than a Jew. He is the Lawgiver for the world; he is a prophet for the church of God. If we know a greater than Moses, this is our distinguished privilege. But though Moses is inferior to Christ, he is not opposed to him. He who truly believes Moses, must believe Christ of whom he wrote, John v. 46; we may learn of Moses, and be the disciples of Jesus; and the very song of heaven will be the song of Moses AND the Lamb, Rev. xv. 3.

CHAPTER II.

EGYPT AND EGYPTIAN HISTORY.

"Lost is thine origin, Mizraim, hid from sight,
Wrapped in the mantle of a rayless night;
Thee, like thy sacred river, none can trace
Back to thy source, or tell the various race
Of each proud monarch." T. C. P.

THE Life of Moses stands at a most important point in history. Just here two great highways of human travel cross each other; here two important ancient nations are brought together; and Moses himself stands related to them both in a most remarkable degree. By birth a native of Egypt; by training acquainted with all the wisdom and learning of that great people; by opportunities invited to a brilliant career of honour and ambition in the high places of the land, such as rarely opens before the youthful mind; he was yet by race, and by cheerful, intelligent choice, a thorough Hebrew; and by the regenerating grace of God, and by faith in the promises given to his fathers, he discerned the true path of duty and honour, of usefulness and renown; and with an energy and perseverance shown by few men and excelled by none, he went steadily forward to that lifework which has justly recorded his name among the greatest benefactors of his people and of the world.

Now we can intelligently consider the life of such a man only when we make ourselves somewhat familiar with the lands, the people, and the times to which he stood so remarkably related. The scenes among which any man lives are intimately connected with our knowledge of the man. It has been said that geography and narrative are like body and spirit; we know the spirit through the matter, in the use of which it makes itself visible. If every student of ancient times should know something of Egypt; if no foreign nation is more frequently mentioned in the Bible, and therefore some acquaintance with their manners and history is requisite to understand what is said of the Israelites themselves; especially must we gain some knowledge of his native land, if we would intelligently follow the footsteps, and understand the character and life of Moses.

Among the sources of geographical information respecting the lands spoken of in the Bible, it is of great interest and importance to remember that the lands themselves still remain. Egypt and Palestine, the Nile and the Red Sea, Goshen and the Desert, Sinai and Pisgah, remain as they were three thousand years ago; but little change has passed over the natural features of those grand lands; the names of many places remain the same, others show that they are derived from the ancient names, and others are associated with the historical events of the Scripture history; and even the habits of the people now living there afford remarkable illustration of the sacred narratives. It is no slight corroborative proof of the strict veracity of the Scriptural writers that they were evidently so familiar with the lands, and the times, and the people they describe. Charges of inaccuracy have indeed been made; but a thorough acquaintance with each particular has invariably proved the Scriptures right, and the carping critics wrong. No lands have been so full of interest to the civilized portion of mankind; none have been so much visited, so often described, so carefully compared with these ancient descriptions. Every traveller there finds the Bible his most indispensable handbook; and no candid man fails to recognize the scenes described in it, and to discern that the writers of Scripture were intimately acquainted with the lands and people of whom they speak.

The Land of Egypt occupies the north-eastern extremity of the continent of Africa; borders upon both the Red and Mediterranean Seas; and having the great Desert of Sahara on the south-west, is divided by the river Nile, flowing from the south to the north. In the Hebrew Scriptures the country is called Mizraim, Gen. xlv. 20, and sometimes the land of Ham, Ps. cvi. 22; cv. Mizraim was a son of Ham, Gen. x. 6, and his descendants first settled

Egypt. Some, however, otherwise derive Mizraim, and suppose that its grammatical form, which is in the dual number, refers to the two parts, Upper and Lower Egypt, into which the country was often divided.* So far as the Scriptural history in the times of Moses is concerned, we have chiefly to do with Lower Egypt. There the Israelites dwelt; and, though during part of their bondage one king may have ruled the entire land, and though some of them may have been sent to labour in Upper Egypt, the scenes of Moses' labours were in Lower Egypt.

Egypt has been long renowned for its large population and the great fertility of its soil. "Herodotus affirms that 20,000 populous cities existed in Egypt during the reign of Amasis; Diodorus calculates 18,000 large villages and towns."† But though we cannot credit either of these statements, it is doubtless true that the ancient population was large. The fertility of the country, which was the result of careful cultivation, and the enriching overflowings of the river Nile, caused the land to receive the name of "the granary of the world." In later times, the wretched government of the country, especially since it has passed under the power of the Turks, has destroyed all enterprise for careful tillage; the fertility of Egypt does not correspond with its ancient reputation, and the population is

* Gesenius makes מצור the singular. Isa. xix. 6. This is doubtful.

† Wilkinson, Abridged Edition, 1, 304.

small. In natural position no country in the world is in advance of Egypt. At the ends of the Red and Mediterranean Seas, it commands the commerce of three continents. It lies directly in the path from all Europe to Persia, India, and China: and there is no better outlet for the great regions of Central Africa than the valley of the Nile. Napoleon thought that Alexander the Great never did a wiser or more politic thing than to found the city of Alexandria; and Napoleon showed his estimate of the political position of Egypt, when he gave his energies to conquer the country, desired to hold it as the key to all the East, and would have laid there the foundation of a great oriental empire.*

Besides the land itself, we have other sources of knowledge respecting ancient Egypt. The main written sources of history are the Scriptures themselves; some fragments that have been preserved of Manetho, an Egyptian priest of more than a thousand years later date than Moses, and a part of whose reputed writings are held to be spurious; and the Greek writers Herodotus, Diodorus, and Eratosthenes. Then we have the existing relics of Egyptian civilization as it once was. The ruins of the country sufficiently prove the former power of their kings; their pyramids have for ages been

* Alison says that Leibnitz urged the conquest of Egypt upon Louis XIV. as the true Key to the great East.—Hist. of Europe, 1st Series, 1, 498.

reckoned among the wonders of the world; and in the paintings yet found there, and in the remains that have been discovered, we have an exhibition almost complete of ancient Egyptian society, as to manners, dress, articles of use and luxury, employments, and pleasures. Evidently the painters of ancient Egypt possessed the art of making indelible colours beyond the skill of modern artists. The paintings on the interior walls of their tombs are as vivid now, after the lapse of thousands of years, as if the colours had been freshly laid on.

In late years learned men have found the key to the hieroglyphic inscriptions upon the Egyptian monuments; and the information gathered from these records of the past, adds to our knowledge of the ancient times. For ages these inscriptions had been illegible; and the study bestowed upon them seemed all vague conjecture. But during the stay of the French in Egypt, at the beginning of this century, a French officer, in digging the foundation of a fort near Rosetta, casually found a broken block of stone, having upon it an inscription, not entirely perfect, but written in three characters. One of these was the sacred, another the common Egyptian character, and the third was the Greek.* As the Greek could be read by scholars,

* This stone is now in the British Museum. The Philomathean Society of the University of Pennsylvania, having received a fac-simile of the stone in plaster, appointed a committee of gentlemen to translate it. The result was a beautiful quarto, the second edition of which, 1859, I have examined with much interest. They have

it enabled learned men to spell out the probable meaning of the others; and finally to arrive at some degree of accuracy in reading the hieroglyphics. Yet there is still much uncertainty as to their true interpretation; scarcely any two scholars agree exactly in reading either names or dates; and the discrepancies, in regard especially to chronology, are wide and irreconcilable.

The history of Egypt, derived from these various sources, is divided into seven periods: 1st, The primitive age from Mizraim to Menes; 2d, The age of the Pharaohs; 3d, The Persians; 4th, The Ptolemies; 5th, The Romans; 6th, The Arabs; and 7th, The Turks. The age that concerns us, in reading the history of Moses, is that during which the Pharaohs ruled in the land. The most fabulous dates have been assigned to this portion of the history by various writers; some extravagantly place the earliest era of Egyptian history 17,000 years back; and some ridiculous blunders have been made by men affecting to be wise in the reading of the monuments. According to Bunsen, the era of Menes was B. C. 3643; Lepsius says 3893; Dr. Seyffarth 2783, and he makes Menes the same as Mizraim; while Sir Gardiner Wilkinson assigns Menes a place among mythical personages, declines

given a picture of the stone itself; a translation of the Greek, Demotic, and Hieroglyphic texts, elegantly embellished; a fac-simile of the Demotic; the text of the Greek; and various notes illustrating the whole. The volume is an elegant specimen of American scholarship and typography.

to mention any date for him, and alleges that no certain era has been established in the early Egyptian chronology. Difficulties on this subject are no new thing. In the days of Augustine, the claims to high antiquity on the part of various nations were disputed; their writings were called in question; the writers were said to "speak what they conjectured (putant), not what they knew;" and Augustine affirmed that the Egyptian years were but four months long.*

The best scholars now admit that the various dynasties assigned to the age of the Pharaohs were not consecutive to each other. The land was divided during at least a large portion of the time; and several kings reigned contemporaneously in different parts of the country. Nor can we judge of the period by the number of the dynasty. For example, the eighth dynasty is arranged after the thirteenth; and the seventh perhaps after the fifteenth or eighteenth. It was perhaps at the commencement of the twelfth dynasty that Egypt was invaded by a nation of foreigners, who held possession of Lower Egypt, and possibly, for a part of the time, of the whole country, for five or six centuries. These are known in history as the Hykshos (Hycsôs), or shepherd kings of Egypt. The shepherds of the fifteenth dynasty were the greatest of the foreign kings; and the fifth king of this dynasty, named Assa, may have been the

* De Civitate Dei, Lib. xii., ch. x.

Pharaoh in whose reign Joseph became the prime minister of the kingdom.

In the seventeenth dynasty, or, as some say, in the eighteenth, or Diospolitan dynasty, the shepherd kings were expelled from Egypt by a different race, who were bitterly opposed to them, and who seized upon their possessions in the eastern part of the Delta. This change of rulers is signified in the words of Moses: "Now there arose up a new king over Egypt, which knew not Joseph." Exod. i. 8. To suppose that this king was of another dynasty, will sufficiently explain the change of policy towards the Israelites. Yet indeed it does not become us to affirm positively touching matters so much in dispute, or to attempt to decide questions where the best informed have no decisive proofs to support their views.

CHAPTER III.

PROVIDENTIAL PREPARATIONS.

"Not first the bright, and after that the dark—
But first the dark, and after that the bright:
First the thick cloud, and then the rainbow's arc;
First the dark grave, then resurrection-light."

BONAR.

THE dwelling-place of the Israelites in Egypt is in the Scriptures called the land of Goshen. Like most other large rivers, the Nile branches off as it approaches the sea, and enters the Mediterranean by various mouths. The portion of land covered by these spreading branches is called the Delta of the river; this term being derived from the Greek letter, Delta, Δ, which such a territory resembles in shape. The most easterly stream thus flowing from the main river is called the Pelusiac arm of the Nile; and upon this, it is supposed, the land of Goshen was situated. This is a fertile part of the country: here Joseph settled his family, by the permission of the reigning Pharaoh: and though some may have been scattered in servitude to more distant parts of Egypt, here the great body of the Israelitish people remained until the period of the Exodus.

Various opinions have been held respecting the length of time spent by the sons of Jacob in the land of Egypt. In Exodus xii. 40, 41, the time of their sojourning there, seems expressly stated to a very day. "Now the sojourning of the children of Israel who dwelt in Egypt, was four hundred and thirty years. And it came to pass at the end of the four hundred and thirty years, even the selfsame day it came to pass, that all the hosts of the Lord went out from the land of Egypt." But the exactness of this statement depends, of course, upon the date from which we begin to reckon. Some have thought four hundred and thirty years much too short a period for so large an increase of the people. Yet the objection amounts to nothing, since the increase is expressly regarded as remarkably rapid; the narrative indeed will bear the construction that it was miraculously so; and the objection is further baseless, if we suppose that the retainers of Jacob, though not expressly mentioned, descended with him to Egypt. Others suppose that four hundred years is quite too long a time.* The true statement, we suppose, is this: that the four hundred and thirty years are to be reckoned from the time when God made a covenant with Abraham, and used two expressions to fix the period of the bondage in a strange land. See Gen. xv. 13–16. His seed was to be afflicted four hun-

* Lepsius says ninety years. Kurtz's Hist. Old Cov. ii. 145. Bunsen, 1434. Smith's Dict. Bible, i. 509.

dred years, and yet to come out in the fourth generation. Four hundred years at that age of the world, was too long a period for four generations. The apostle Paul reconciles the two expressions when he teaches us explicitly, that the four hundred and thirty years extend from the promise to the law, Gal. iii. 17; that is, from the covenant of Abraham to the giving of the law on Sinai. The actual stay in Egypt is exactly half of the four hundred and thirty years. The first half may be thus reckoned:

From the promise to Isaac's birth* . .	25
At Jacob's birth Isaac's age was† . .	60
Jacob's age on going to Egypt was‡ . .	130
	215

As Joseph's age is known, and we know that he lived seventy-one years in Egypt after his father came down;§ and as Moses was eighty years old at the Exodus;|| we ascertain that a period of sixty-four years intervened between the death of Joseph and the birth of Moses.

There are some matters of interesting inquiry respecting the stay of the Israelites in the land of Egypt, to which our thoughts may properly turn. Why did they remain there for so long a time; what was their condition there; and what effects

* Gen. xii. 4; xxi. 5. † Gen. xxv. 26. ‡ Gen. xlvii. 9.

§ Comp. Gen. xli. 46–53; xlv. 11; l. 26.

|| Exod. vii. 7; Acts vii. 23–30.

were produced upon them, by the bondage of Egypt and by intercourse with a people that were highly civilized and yet grossly idolatrous? are inquiries we should not wholly omit. We would have supposed that Jacob and his sons would wish to return early to Canaan. They had originally gone to Egypt as a refuge from the prevailing famine; they doubtless designed to remain only during the pressure of this calamity. Yet even Jacob, with all his attachments to Canaan, especially as the promised land, remained seventeen years in this strange country, and died there: and his children yet sojourned there for four generations.

Perhaps the warm attachment of the venerable patriarch for the beloved Joseph, was the first cord that fastened the tribes of Israel to the land of Egypt. Twenty years before, he had been rudely separated from this favourite child; he had mourned him as among the dead by a cruel death; and now, after his long sorrow, in a time of peculiar distress, Joseph had been restored to him. And the circumstances of his history, proving God's special favour for Israel's deliverance; the excellency of his character, as the matured fruit of his early loveliness; the high respect and influence he had gained in Egypt; and the quiet, and plenty, and comfort he provided for his aged parent after so many years of toil and grief;—all these things served to attach the loving father to such a son: and we cannot wonder that thenceforward Jacob could not bear the thought of another, and especially of a voluntary separation. Around Joseph clung the father's warm affections; and he and his sons were equally dependent upon this Ruler in Egypt. The time had come for the fulfilment of Joseph's early dreams. The sun, and moon, and eleven stars pay their homage to him; and all the sheaves of the house of Israel bow down before him. Gen. xxxvii. 7–9.

Doubtless other reasons joined to detain the Israelites in Egypt. The land of Goshen was fertile; the Egyptians honoured them as the brethren of their deliverers; Joseph was held in high regard in the land: and he wished them to share in the prosperity that Providence had given him. Perhaps, also, there were providential indications of their duty to remain still in Egypt; the way was not open for their return; and without charging them with indifference to Canaan, or to the covenant with Abraham, we may quite justify, or nearly justify their long stay in this foreign land. The predicted time of their stay as given to Abraham may have been considered authoritative of their duty, as its approaching end gave them hopes of deliverance. But all this while the best of the people had no thought of giving up Canaan, or of remaining in Egypt. The burial of Jacob, and even of all the patriarchs in the promised land, Acts vii. 15, 16; and the oath which Joseph exacted that they should carry up his bones, all serve to show their attachment to the covenant of Abraham; and prove that they kept constantly before their minds that Egypt was a foreign land, and that they were sojourners there. Joseph's oath would keep them from forming undue attachments to Egypt; and would serve to remind them that that was not their home. And thus we may notice, that from the very beginning of their national history, the Jews have possessed that trait of character, which is so plainly yet to be seen in them, after the lapse of thirty-five centuries; the capability of existing among other nations still a distinct race, without laws, rulers, or lands of their own.

But besides all the other reasons, known and unknown, for the long stay of the people in Egypt, we are expressly told that Divine Providence had a purpose to serve, in regard to the inhabitants of Canaan. That land was divinely selected as the residence of the chosen people; and this perhaps with special reference to its geographical position, surrounded by the chief historical nations of the world, and fitted, through idolatrous ages, to keep before men a testimony for the true God. But before the call of Abraham, this territory was occupied by the Canaanitish tribes; and their title of actual possession, the providence of God would not hastily, nor without due reason, strike aside. While then the sons of Abraham were too few in numbers to occupy this whole land; and while they were passing through a state of preparatory discipline, God was exercising his forbearance towards the wicked tribes of Canaan. But every call to repentance, they refused to hear; and even the terrible overthrow of Sodom and Gomorrah, wrought no permanent and salutary impressions. During the stay of Israel in Egypt, the tribes in Palestine were declining in morals, apostatizing in religion, and ripening for destruction. Great corruptions prevailed among them from the earliest accounts we possess. Piety had not yet died out in the days of Abraham, as we learn from the eminent example of Melchizedek. But the people of the land at large, refused to be influenced by Abraham and by Melchizedek, as the Sodomites rejected Lot; and they went on to fill up the cup of their iniquity.

We have in this whole matter an important example of that truth, so hard for man fully to comprehend, and yet so frequently brought to our notice in the Scriptures, that the sovereign purposes of God, as the Providential Ruler, do in no wise interfere with the exercise of man's freest agency even in evil; and that righteousness governs all God's dealings with the sons of men. Here were tribes of wicked men, deserving God's judgments, and feeling enough of them to awaken repentance, if they were disposed to repent. Yet they were not wholly wicked. When Abraham plead with God to save Sodom, the foundation of his plea was the hope that a few righteous men remained among them; and the assurance that the Judge of all the earth would do right. Gen. xviii. 25. God had forbearance with the Canaanites so long as a few remained among them maintaining his fear; it was because they did not like to retain him in their knowledge that he gave them up to walk in their own ways, Rom. i. 28; and in despite of all his long-suffering, their iniquity increased. Even to give his suffering people their promised rest, he would not prematurely drive out the Canaanites, until by their iniquity his wrath was ripened. In the increasing and ripening abominations of the tribes of Canaan, we have, on the one hand, one of the reasons for the long sojourn of the sons of Jacob in a strange and oppressive land; and on the other, we have the providential justification of the exterminating warfare afterwards waged by Joshua: Gen. xv. 16.

Forbearance with human sinfulness, yet the just judgments of God against incorrigible wickedness, in nations or in individuals, may be read in all the past pages of history. Read the records of the nations, and amid all the varying scenes and circumstances and agencies of Providence, the same principles govern the Divine administration. God's holy law binds men everywhere and always. Neither nations nor men can sin with impunity. And we should not misunderstand the long delays of Divine judgments. It is not that God forgets; much less that he approves. The true secret is that he forbears. He is slack neither concerning his laws, nor concerning his promises, but is long-suffering towards men; not willing that any should perish, but that all should come to repentance, 2 Pet. iii. 9. And we, who live in a land and age pre-eminently instructed both in the law of God and in the gospel of Christ, should wisely know our times and fear to abuse the Divine forbearance by continuance in evil.

CHAPTER IV.

THE BONDAGE OF EGYPT.

"When hang the heavy clouds above
 And Israel Egypt's burdens bears,
The God of Abraham looks in love,
 And hears his people's anguished prayers;
The heavier cross calls forth their cry,
And when they plead His aid is nigh."

We have no means of ascertaining at what period a change took place in the circumstances of the Israelites. The seventy remaining years of Joseph's life, after his brethren came to Egypt, were doubtless spent in peace and prosperity; and as yet perhaps, no dark clouds threatened the coming storm. And if we consider together these two things—their condition in Egypt, and the influence produced upon them by their stay there—it would be no strange thing in human experience, even in pious experience, if these prosperous years were the most dangerous years of their sojourn. In the favour of the Egyptians, in the fertility of Goshen, in the sensual pleasures of an idolatrous religion, lay concealed the seductions which might lull them into forgetfulness of Canaan, of the covenant of

Abraham, and of the pure worship of the living God. Perhaps to save them from deeper declinings, the dark period of Israelitish history in the Bondage was in the mercy of their covenant God. This is the happiness of God's people, that trouble never comes by chance; and that its severest power but results in the more precious blessings.

> "The clouds we so much dread
> Are big with mercy."

The troubles of the people began upon the accession of a new king, who either knew not Joseph's services, or did not regard them as demanding his gratitude. The language, as before suggested, refers, in all probability, to a new dynasty. Some suppose that this was not a dynasty of the shepherd kings; and in this they find a plausible reason for their readiness to oppress a race of shepherds, like the sons of Jacob. Yet even a new dynasty of the same race, knowing that the Israelites had been the friends and supporters of their predecessors, might for this reason treat them with rigour. And evidently it was no design of the new king to drive the Israelites from Egypt. This he would have done, had he regarded them as invaders, whose presence was dangerous to the permanence of his throne. One avowed object of the oppression was to keep them from "getting up out of the land." Ex. i. 10. The language implies that the expectation of departure on the part of this people was well known, and plainly kept both before their own minds and before the minds of the Egyptians. The king expresses no fear that they will fight and rule Egypt; but that they may join others merely to facilitate their own escape. Perhaps this is proof of the degradation of Israel, as compared with the high civilization of Egypt, that not dominion, but escape, is feared; and that slavery, and not expulsion, is the remedy sought.

These fears were specially aroused by the great increase of the people. Josephus, however, declares that the king was led to adopt severe measures, and especially to issue the decree that the male children should be destroyed, by the prediction of one of their wise men that a child should be born who would raise the Israelites, and cast down the Egyptians. But this, together with many other Jewish and Mohammedan fables respecting Moses and his wonderful character, we may regard as the offspring of man's desire to render more marvellous the great doings of God. Let it suffice us to know that measures of oppression continued, not all the time with equal severity, for perhaps an entire century; and let us notice the engagements of the people in this bondage, and the influence produced upon them by it.

Josephus says, concerning the employments of the Israelites, that the Egyptians set them to cut channels for the river; to build levees for the banks, walls for their cities, and the pyramids; to learn all sorts of mechanical arts; and to do various kinds of hard labour.* It is likely that they were engaged in all these things. The chief objection to the statement that they built the pyramids is found in the fact that these structures are almost all stone, though a few are found of brick. Possibly the time of building the pyramids may not agree with the period of the Bondage; but the terms of the sacred narrative do not forbid us to believe that they may have wrought both in stone and brick. This we know, that labours in the field and the making of brick formed a part of their toils. It is difficult alike to determine what cities are designated by the names Pithom and Raamses, and what is the meaning of the term "treasure cities" as applied to them.

The writings of travellers and of orientalists, especially since so many explorations have been made of Egyptian antiquities, afford us many interesting illustrations of the labours of the people during this period. It is a matter of wonder to many readers of the Bible why the Israelites needed straw to aid them in making brick. The solution is very simple. In an atmosphere of wonderful salubrity; in a land where rain very seldom falls, and where fuel is very scarce, bricks dried or baked in a kiln are but little known.† Eastern bricks

* Josephus Antiq. ii. 9, § 1.

† "There is no evidence that the Egyptians in early times used any but crude brick, a burnt brick being as sure a record of the Roman dominion as an imperial coin." Reginald Stuart Poole, in Smith's Dict. Bible, ii. 542.

are *sun-dried.* Even in Texas and Central America *adobes,* or unburnt brick, are used in building houses; they cost nothing but a little labour, and yet are of extraordinary durability.* Straw was mixed with the Egyptian bricks to make them stick better together; but no straw was needed except for those formed from the mud or alluvial deposits of the Nile. Bricks made three thousand years ago,† with and without straw, are now found with the names of the monarchs, in whose reigns they were made, stamped upon them.

Mr. Wilkinson thinks that it is unreasonable to look for any sculptures representing the Hebrews among the remains of Egyptian antiquity, since no remains are found in that part of Egypt where they lived; but other foreign captives are found on the monuments "occupied in the same manner, overlooked by similar 'taskmasters,' and performing the very same labours, as the Israelites described in the Bible."‡ Others, however, think that some of the Israelites may have been sent to labour in Upper Egypt. In Exod. v. 12, we read, "So the people were scattered abroad throughout all the land of Egypt." Rosellini, an Italian antiquary, sent out by the Tuscan Government with the French commission under Champollion, took fifteen hundred drawings from the Egyptian monuments, and published a splendid work upon the

* New Am. Cyc. Art. Adobe Houses. † Wilkinson, ii. 194.
‡ Wilkinson, ii. 195.

subject. He found, painted upon the walls of a tomb at Thebes, a representation which has excited great interest among scholars, and which he regards as a "picture representing the Hebrews as they were engaged in making brick." In this picture some labourers are carrying clay and bricks, some mixing, others moulding, the clay; the task-masters are easily distinguished. The complexion and physiognomy determine the labourers to be Hebrews, and the taskmasters to be Egyptians.* The only objection to the application of this picture to the Hebrews is, that it was found at Thebes; and we have no certain proof that they were ever there. But it may, at all events, illustrate the kind of labour to which the Egyptians put their bondsmen. As it was the proud boast of their kings that no Egyptian had put forth his hand to erect their monuments,† we may easily believe that they would make the Israelites serve them with rigour.

But these labours of the sons of Jacob were not useless to them. They were indeed down-trodden and degraded, but they must have gained various elements of Egyptian civilization. They went down to Egypt merely a race of shepherds. When they came out, they still possessed cattle; especially some of the tribes, Num. xxxii. 1–4; but in an agricultural country like Egypt, the main body

* Hengstenberg's Egypt and the Books of Moses, 81.

† Diodorus Siculus in Wiseman's Lectures, 268, Hengstenberg, 80.

of the people became cultivators of the soil, as they were to remain in Palestine. So we find them complaining in the desert for want of the garden vegetables they had enjoyed in Egypt, Num. xi. 5. And doubtless they learned useful trades and arts: not only building, but weaving linen, tapestry, and fine clothes; working in precious metals and stones; and various other arts: as we learn from the erection of the tabernacle in the wilderness. So the promise made to Abraham that they should come out "with great substance" was "fulfilled in a much higher sense than by their coming out of Egypt with vessels of gold and silver."* Gen. xv. 14; Ex. xii. 35, 36.

But what was the moral and religious influence of the Bondage upon the sons of Abraham? is a much more important inquiry. If we may judge by that generation which Moses led into the desert, we cannot give a favourable reply. They became entangled in Egyptian pollutions, and enamoured of Egyptian idolatry; so that even the wonders of the Exodus and of Sinai could not win them back to the God who did so much for them, or save them from falling beneath his wrath on their way to Canaan. It may be that the Israelites were not allowed the full exercise of their religion in the land of Egypt, and that the decline of piety among them was the consequence of this. "Herodotus expressly tells us that the Egyptians esteemed it a

* Kurtz's Hist. Old Cov., ii. 168.

profanation to sacrifice any kind of cattle except swine, bulls, clean calves, and geese; and in another place that heifers, rams, and goats were held sacred either in one province or in another."* This seems to correspond with what Moses declared to Pharaoh, that he could not offer sacrifices in the land: "Lo, shall we sacrifice the abomination of the Egyptians before their eyes, and will they not stone us?" Exodus viii. 26.

It is very evident from the history subsequently, that many of the people of Israel became entangled in the idolatries of Egypt. Scarcely anything is more remarkable than the fact, that the Jews so easily degenerated into idolaters at any time previous to the Babylonish captivity; and yet that they have never been betrayed into idolatry by all their trials and persecutions since that time. The making of the golden calf at Sinai seems evidently to have been the fruit of the lessons learned in Egypt. The god Apis bore the form of an ox or bull among the Egyptians; and the golden calf was doubtless an imitation of this. Perhaps many other of the defilements and temptations of the desert had a similar origin. It seems lamentable to reflect that, with very few honourable exceptions, the entire body of the people, who had reached adult years before leaving Egypt, were so corrupted by the Egyptian manners, that they were unfit to enter Canaan: and that a new generation, of those

* Warburton's Div. Legation of Moses, ii. 156.

who were young enough to receive salutary and lasting impressions from the great wonders which God wrought in Egypt, and at the Red Sea, and in the desert, must be trained up for the service of God before the promises made to Abraham could receive their fulfilment.

Yet we need not suppose that the corruption was total. Even some of those who perished in the journey may have possessed a measure of piety. And there were others of more consistent and firmer faith. Perhaps that word is true of every time of distress among God's people, as of the days of Elijah and Paul, that a remnant of God's people are faithful to him. Rom. xi. 5. Afflictions not only try but winnow the church. There are fewer professors of piety in times of distress: but they who are faithful, are as the finest of the wheat. We may doubtless reckon among the faithful few, the parents of Moses. They looked for the fulfilment of the promise made to Abraham, and kept firm their confidence in God in despite of the king's commandment. The remembrance of Joseph, and the solemn oath which bound each succeeding generation to carry him up with them in their anticipated Exodus, may have exerted a salutary influence during those years of darkness.

The Jews have a proverb, "When the tale of bricks is doubled, then comes Moses." The meaning of it is similar to the words we often use, "Man's extremity is God's opportunity." We wonder that God's chosen people are called to bear so much. How long he tries our faith! How far, sometimes, do his people stray! Yet all is beneath his eye. He is not unmindful. He hears their groaning: he sees their affliction: his appearance to save is certain: and shall be "in the self-same day" of a wisely appointed purpose. Ex. xii. 41. And this much we know, that the heavy hand of Egypt called forth the prayers of Israel towards their God: and the seed of Jacob never sought his face in vain. Exodus ii. 23. Isa. xlv. 19.

CHAPTER V.

PARENTAL FAITH.

"All other passions change
With changing circumstances: rise or fall
Dependent on their object: claim returns;
Live on reciprocation; and expire
Unfed by hope. A mother's fondness reigns
Without a rival, and without an end." H. MORE.

IF we could look in upon the humble dwellings of the sons of Israel when the cruel edict of Pharaoh was made known, we might not only see the signs of distress, but the tokens of renewed devotion in the presence of their covenant God. Jehovah saw their affliction, heard their cry, and knew their sorrows. Ex. iii. 7. Indeed it may appear that this very decree, which was not long rigidly enforced, was permitted in his holy providence, that the future deliverer of Israel might be thrown for his education and training upon their care, who could best fit him for coming duties. Moses was not the first-born son of his parents. Aaron was three years his senior; and as no mention is made of his peril, it is likely that the short-lived law was proclaimed just before the birth of Moses. The decree filled the hearts of these pious parents with anguish. An event usually anticipated with joy is expected now with sorrow: yet that was a blessed strength of piety which led this humble pair to brave the penalty of disobedience.

"They saw that Moses was a proper child," says the apostle. Reference may here be made to more than ordinary personal beauty in Moses, which the Jews do not fail to exalt, which even the Scriptures mention, and which Josephus greatly praises. Acts vii. 20. Or the expression may refer to some impression upon the minds of his parents that by him God would bring Israel's promised deliverance. That "they were not afraid of the king's commandment:" Heb. xi. 23, is a declaration not designed to deny that they had those natural fears and misgivings which frequently co-exist with the firmest confidence; and which indeed exhibit, not the weakness, but the strength of faith. The strength of faith is magnified by its steadfast exercise in spite of the most formidable difficulties: difficulties not despised, but fully realized, and sensibly felt; and yet firmly resisted, and finally overcome.

The parents of Moses knew the decree of Pharaoh; and they could not be indifferent to its cruel terms. They often thought of the expecting crocodile on the reedy border of the Nile; they often trembled lest the ear of a passing Egyptian should catch the sound of his infantile cries, and search their scanty stuff to find the darling boy; they guarded carefully by day, they watched anxiously through the darkness, for the safety of their hidden charge. It is in human nature that a child born at such a season, and preserved at such hazards, should be so much the more a darling, because in his innocent helplessness he made such demands upon the best affections of the household.

Let the Christian mother, who often surrounds her peaceful, slumbering infant with a thousand imaginary troubles, estimate, if possible, the perplexing anxieties of the mother of Moses, during these three months of watchfulness. In a country where rain scarcely ever falls, and where people sleep in the open air the greater part of the year, and do the most, even of their household work, out of doors, four walls with a flat roof of palm branches, overlaid with mats and plastered with mud, make up a poor man's house.* Had the parents of Moses dwelt in a palace, they might have concealed their child longer; but in the hut of a Hebrew bondman, exposed to intrusion from any passing Egyptian, it was faith indeed that could venture for three months to withstand the order of Pharaoh. And they felt that every day the danger of discovery was greater; that soon the unconscious child would begin to notice the world around him; that soon he must be amused with the trinkets of childhood; that soon he must be allowed first to creep, and then with tottering steps to go forth beyond the narrow

* Sir G. Wilkinson. Ch. 1.

threshold; and thus that every week was one of increasing jeopardy for his life and for the safety of the family. It became obvious to the parents that they must adopt some new means for his preservation; that if faith prompted his early hiding in their humble abode, it could be only presumption that in later months would venture to retain him there; and that between the presumptuous determination to retain their boy and the cowardly desperation that would yield him up, there was due room for the exercise of a wise and intelligent and holy faith in God.

But faith in God is never an idle or heartless principle; and in the exercise of it, the parents of Moses must both work and venture. It was, we naturally judge, with deep solicitude; and we can scarcely doubt, with earnest prayer; and, we are certain upon the testimony of the Scriptures, in the exercise of a well-founded faith, that their changing plan was matured. It exactly met the exigency; and yet to the eye of sense it seemed desperately embraced. Let us not think that their misgivings of evil and apprehensions of danger, disprove their steadfast purpose, or the firmness of their faith in God. The little needle that directs the mariner upon his way is never at rest: it is especially agitated when the ship is tossed by a tempest; yet with all its restlessness there is one point past which it vibrates, and towards which its tendencies constantly are; and that point can as easily be discerned by a practised eye, as if the needle pointed only there. The faith of a human soul will usually have its fears and hopes, its sorrows and joys, its elevations and depressions; but amidst them all, it is not difficult to discover the true bent of the pious mind.

The mother of Moses sought materials for her dreaded but believing task. Upon the borders of the Nile there grows a kind of rush, called in the Scriptures the paper reed, Isa. xix. 7; because long used in the manufacture of paper. Of this same reed, sail cloth, cordage, and even the small boats upon the Nile are still made; and they are yet prevented from leaking by the daubings of slime and pitch.* This plant was sometimes called "biblos," from which comes our word Bible; and "papyrus," from which is our word paper. Plutarch gives it as the "current Egyptian belief that that plant was a protection from crocodiles."†

Such materials ready to her hand, furnished the believing woman with the means to construct a little ark, that her boy might be hidden in the margin of the river. Surely never before nor since has such a vessel carried such a freight. Apart from the exercise of faith in God, the adventure is desperate; but faith can not only excuse, but vindicate

*Land and Book, 1, 336. Wilkinson ii. 95, seq. Smith's Dict. Bible, 1, 498, says that now the papyrus is almost or quite unknown in Egypt: Lowth and Alexander do not refer Isa. xix. 7 to it.

†Stanley's Jewish Church.

this apparent recklessness. There is just ground here for faith. For not only might we say, better the monsters of the Nile than the cruel monarch of Egypt; but we are expressly assured that the ark was resorted to only "when she could no longer hide" the child. Ex. ii. 3. And if the frail vessel should perish, it would be no worse than the discovery of the babe in his mother's arms. It is worthy of remark, that in the sacred Scriptures faith is frequently represented as venturing the soul upon the providence, and, in the most important cases, upon the grace of God, in circumstances that seem desperate whichever way else we turn. The Israelites at the Red Sea seemed hemmed in on every side; Queen Esther pondered the perils of venturing, or of fearing to approach the king; death threatened the Samaritan lepers whether they sat still, or went forth to the hostile camp; and the trembling sinner, afraid that Christ will reject his humble pleading, will but realize his worst fears if he allows them to keep him from the footstool of Divine mercy.

The precious burden entrusted to that slender vessel had a guardianship the most powerful. The plan of that exposure amidst the bulrushes was conceived by parental faith, after united wrestlings with God, comparable, perhaps, to the strivings of their father Jacob at Penuel. Day after day as the believing father bent over his rigorous task in the fields of Egypt, there was a heavier burden on his heart; and his frequent falling tears were only outnumbered by his warmer ascending prayers for the lovely babe. Hour after hour the believing mother snatched the precious but secret moments to weave the rushes for her infant's cradle. But it could not be a speedy task. Many a time, we may imagine, did her hand stay, as she thought that her care for her fondling must give place to the rocking of the wave; her song to the babble of the billow; her warm embrace to the chill bosom of the river; perhaps her fond kiss to the fierce jaw of the monster. Many a time the work was laid aside, and the babe snatched convulsively to that heart from which, it seemed to her, no king could be cruel enough to tear it. But faith took up again the sorrowful but needful work; and with an earnest prayer over every bending of the reeds, she completed her little boat for its perilous place. Truly we should well endure the trials of our times, when we see the conflict of these believing hearts. Faith concealed the babe; faith conceived the plan for his deliverance; faith wove the network of the boat, and the prayers that interlaced its sides were thicker than the reeds; faith chose the place and the hour of depositing its charge by the river; and neglectful of nothing that believing hearts or earnest hands could do, faith selected a sentinel, whose warm affection and ready intelligence could be fully trusted; yet whose age and innocence would least excite prejudice or suspicion.

Thus far faith has done well. The ark is finished; the slumbering babe is laid within it; the strong arm of the Hebrew father, forcing himself to composure for others' sake, has laid him by the brink of the water; the weeping mother has taken a parting kiss, and torn herself away; and the little sister is the sole human watcher of the sleeping boy. Faith has done all its work, save one, the last thing; the great connecting bond which secures the blessing upon all the rest. Faith has secured the victory; for it has left the future Deliverer of Israel to the guardianship of God.

CHAPTER VI.

THE EDUCATION OF MOSES.

"Oh worse exchange for death if he should learn
In yon proud palace to disown His hand
Who thus has saved him! Should he e'er embrace,
As sure he will, if bred in Pharaoh's court,
The gross idolatries which Egypt owns;
Then shall I wish he had not been preserved
To shame his fathers, and deny his faith." H. MORE.

IT is wonderfully true in the operations of God's providence that his purposes are accomplished in darkness. The most important events, for the individual believer and for God's suffering church, are often brought about by means that seem to prepare the most opposite and adverse results. The child Moses, was placed in the ark of bulrushes for fear of Pharaoh; and if human wit had been consulted, the daughter of the king would not have been his discoverer, nor the palace of the monarch his refuge.

Yet for that child there are designs in Providence that can be secured only when his foster parent stands thus related to Egypt's throne. There must be *protection* afforded to the foundling that no authority in Egypt can invade. He must be *educated* with *advantages for the cultivation of his mind,* over which no man in that age could claim any superiority; he must have *intercourse with polished society*, and *familiarity with political events and political duties*, such as could be acquired only when he was an honoured inmate of the most refined and intelligent court upon earth. These demands of Providence for the training of the future lawgiver of the Jews, could best be met by leading the daughter of Pharaoh to the margin of the Nile, and by touching her tender feelings by the timely weeping of the Hebrew babe.

But there is another providential design for Moses, superior to all the rest, in his entire education; and if this be lost sight of, the most thorough training in other respects is far worse than useless. What are the advantages of rank and wealth; what the most thorough cultivation of the intellect; what the utmost refinement of manners, if the heart is neglected? The education that does not include the trainings, the attractions and the restraints of virtue, may but strengthen the unruly mind for larger achievements of malice and wickedness. What a calamity it had been, if Moses, the child of Hebrew piety, had been rescued by the daughter of that idolatrous king, to be tutored in the falsehoods and impurity of the Egyptian theology: if his great intellect had been occupied simply with Egyptian learning; if his executive and military abilities had been enlisted to strengthen the despotism of the Egyptian throne; and, if, riveting the chains he should break off, he had risen up as a renegade oppressor of those poor brethren, to whom he was connected by ties of blood; but from whom he was separated by education, by religious training, by the swelling pride of fortuitous station, and by the graspings of ambition in an unholy mind! Better far had the son of Amram been smothered at his birth, or seized by the oppressive law, or swallowed up in the Nile, than be thus nurtured in Pharaoh's house, in his religion, and to the practice of his cruelty.

The providential designs for the education of this favoured child include a moral training, in full keeping with all he was to receive of physical, civil and intellectual. Moses, the Hebrew foundling, might be best protected by the daughter of the Egyptian monarch. Moses, the civilian, might be best educated in the Egyptian court. Moses, the warrior and the leader of Israel's hosts, might best be trained to command large bodies of men in the Egyptian camp: Acts vii. 22. But Moses, in his highest character, the holy man, the prophet of Israel, and the servant of the Lord, must early receive the most important part of his training in the humble abode of his Hebrew parents, where thankful adoration was paid to Jacob's God; where renewed consecration would spring up from his restoration to their embrace; and where every hour he might breathe an atmosphere of faith and prayer. How simple, yet how efficient the agency to reach this end! The silver voice of a girl is heard by the side of the royal damsel, and the ready intelligence of Miriam has secured the blessing most to be desired. The mother of the babe becomes his nurse.

Taught by the word and the providence of God, we should learn to place a high estimate upon the earliest inculcation of religious truth upon the minds of children. When we see in every part of this narrative that the God of providence secures each designed and necessary result through appropriate human instrumentality, we have no just reason to believe that the sterling and decided piety of Moses had its origin in miraculous interposition, apart from the ordinary means of grace. And where else than in the abode of parental piety, and in his early life, did Moses become acquainted with the covenant God of Israel? It is plain, from the first circumstance that occurred on his return to Egypt, that to his brother Aaron he was no stranger. We do not know how long he was allowed to remain with his Hebrew nurse. Doubtless the daughter of Pharaoh was willingly relieved of the attentions which childhood demands, and which it frequently taxes the strongest parental love adequately to supply; and thus the lad was left with his mother during a period quite beyond the helplessness of infancy.

And if we can trace the piety of Moses to parental faithfulness, we may not only find encouragement for the careful discharge of duty, but we may believe also, from such an example, that the task of a pious parent cannot be too soon begun. What a privilege for a child to dwell in a household of piety and prayer! What a responsibility for a parent when it is otherwise! When a child first awakes to notice the things around him, let the serious stated gathering for household devotion become a familiar object. When he first lisps the syllables of articulate language, let his eyes be directed upward, and his tongue taught to say, "Our Father;" let the first names, out of the family circle, that greet his ears, be the names of those holy men of old, whose records are upon the sacred page; and let all his training consist with the culture of an immortal, rational, moral being. Teach him of his own sinfulness; point him for its pardon to the Great Redeemer; and impress upon him the importance of living for God's glory here, and for his enjoyment hereafter. The parent who can neglect these teachings, or who fails to mingle with them the frequent and fervent prayers of an earnest heart, and to enforce them by the power of a holy life, is recreant to his very noblest duties.

Let us not be told that you love your child when you have given him a comfortable home; when you have clothed him in apparel befitting his station; when you have liberally provided for the cultivation of his mind; and when you have set before him your own example, as a man of industry and integrity and truth. All these things you may do, and yet the very best cultivation of the heart, and the highest preparation of the soul for usefulness to man and for glory to God, may be omitted. And to omit these things is to promote their opposite. The child untrained to godliness is trained to ungodliness; the influence withheld from the cause of Christ is used against it; and all the advantages otherwise bestowed upon your child, will but increase his responsibilities and yours, if through your neglect of his moral training, his influence in life is pernicious, and his soul is finally lost. How much depends, for the safety of the best ship that ever sailed, upon the hand that guides the helm; for if the pilot is bent upon mischief, the very size and swiftness of the vessel, and all her superiority, in the number of her passengers and the value of her cargo, will but enable him to make her shipwreck more disastrous. A few years ago, according to the current statements in the papers of the time, the captain of a noble steamship upon the Atlantic gave evident tokens of insanity; and was detected in an attempt to run the ship ashore. And you can easily imagine the condition of the passengers, had his indisposition remained unperceived. Surrounded by many comforts, even provided with many luxuries for their voyage; moved forward against wind and current by the energy of mighty machinery; exulting in the swiftness with which they were hurried across the waste of waters, they knew not that these mighty forces were fearfully controlled by a hostile power, and that in any unexpected moment the majestic fabric might be directed to certain destruction.

Even more dreadful than this, is the conception of an immortal mind, which, with all its inherent and acquired excellencies, is swayed by the madness of estrangement from virtue, and of hostility to God. The more powerful and cultivated is the mind of your child, the better his standing of rank and wealth in society, the larger his sphere of influence; in all these things so much the worse, if the heart is not schooled to piety, if the will is wayward, if the conscience is defiled. Far better neglect any other thing, even every other thing in instruction, than the education of the heart to piety. The conscience is the pilot of that noble ship sent forth under your care for an immortal voyage; and can you store and equip that vessel so careless of the guide by which she must be directed to the haven of eternal rest, or misdirected into the great gulf stream of perdition?

The parental responsibility of thus caring for and promoting the moral training of each child, is the greater for one obvious reflection, already suggested to every thoughtful mind. In the vast majority of cases, it is not within the parent's power to mature and effect wise and judicious plans for the liberal education of his family. If the entire education of Moses had been intrusted to his natural guardians, they could not have fitted him for the high station he was afterwards to fill. Himself bound to obey his Egyptian task-masters, Amram had no power to lift his son above his own servile condition. And many a parent now can scarcely clothe and feed, much less educate his children as his heart longs to do. But it is a high consolation to know that the very best portion of a child's education may be given, let the worldly circumstances of the parent be as they may. The humble father may be able to feed his little ones with but a scanty portion, and to cover them with but tattered rags; and yet nothing hinders but that beneath his lowly roof there may be a process of education going forward, which shall better fit his children for the stirring duties of life, and for the scenes of the judgment-day, than the splendid apparelling and the profuse education of those born in many a palace. If the heart of that poverty-stricken parent is itself right in the sight of God, he is possessed of riches for his child's inheritance, with which the mines of California may not be compared. Nothing hinders but that from the open pages of inspiration he may guide the conscience of his immortal pupil into the wisdom of God. If he is often oppressed by a sense of his own ignorance and incompetency to discharge duties like these, there is access to the mercy seat of a gracious God, as free beneath his roof as in the vaulted aisles of the noblest temple. The Holy Spirit of God visits the abode of the humble; the Redeemer's personal ministry was among the poor; and many, even as lowly as the beggar Lazarus, Luke xvi., are the objects of angelic care and the heirs of eternal glory.

Oh, Christian parent! whatever else you may lack; though your child may be meanly dressed; though you must early send him forth to labour for his livelihood, deprived of the advantages of a thorough education; yet God has given you favourable and abundant opportunities to educate the heart. You have the most important time and the most important part of his training in your own hands, as no one else can have it; and much responsibility rests upon you, that he may be sent forth prepared to live aright. The chief end of life may be gained as truly by a short earthly career as by a long one; by a poor man as by a rich one; without a learned education as with it. The humble flower is God's work, and shows his glory, and stands where he placed it, as truly as the giant oak that overshadows it. Let but the heart be right in the sight of God, and the weakness of our arm, the poverty of our resources, the narrowness of our influence, and the shortness of our life shall be no barrier to the final approval: "Well done, thou good and faithful servant." Let parents, pious or ungodly, see here their responsibility. You shall not be called to an account before God for serious guilt, should your child fail to become rich in gold, or high in influence and power over men; but it is not likely that you can be wholly guiltless, if your son is lacking in moral principle, and if the chosen course of his life is aside from the paths of virtue and piety.

We may well imagine with what anxiety and solicitude the parents of this Hebrew child looked forward to the period when he should be separated from them, and go to be, perhaps, the spoiled and pampered favourite of the palace. We instinctively recognize that every part of his education, so far as he was intrusted to the parental control, was given with reference to the trials and temptations which were known to be but a little in advance of him; and as his early years passed rapidly away, there was an increasing solicitude for the unknown moment when the king's daughter would claim her charge. Truly the training of Moses was a constant source of anxiety to his parents. We judge that often the fond mother cast forward her thoughts in a vain attempt to anticipate the events of succeeding years; and knowing, as she did, some of the temptations of a heathen court, no doubt her fervent prayers ascended that when her child was addressed by the flattering splendours of the palace, he might not forget the humble dwelling of parental love; that with him the gorgeous ritual of paganism might not be more attractive than the simple services of patriarchal piety; that the sensual temptations of a corrupt people might not lead him to forget his early lessons of honour and purity. What parent, alive to the true welfare of the soul, would not tremble to send forth a young lad, where he would be so likely to forget, and even to despise parental care and parental piety; and where so many and so strong temptations might influence him to apostasy from Israel's covenant God?

And yet the anxiety of this Hebrew household but represents the solicitude that may fill the mind of every thoughtful parent. Did these parents anticipate the dreaded hour when another roof must shelter their child, when another mind would control him, when other influences would educate him, when other scenes would be around him, beyond their knowledge and far from all they would wish or approve? And may not similar anxieties fill the breast of every parent, to make him earnest in embracing his present opportunities of influencing his child, lest each successive day may be the last? It is not only the thought that your child may be torn from your fond embrace. There is the reflection, even more serious, to quicken you in your parental duty, that you may yourself be removed from earth. Before another month the officers of the law may appoint other guardians to educate your children. They may be placed in circumstances very different from what you would desire. Not a parent among us can tell who shall complete the training we have but begun for our little ones. It is with us all, as with the parents of Moses, that in faith, and with prayer and diligent earnestness, we are to embrace the opportunities we now have; for we know not at what hour we must resign our unfinished task to other hands.

Nor should we relax our energies or remit our care, in the cheerful prospect that we and our children may be spared together, until they enter on life's mature and serious duties. For when we are spared as long as a parent may hope to be; when we have done all that it is a parent's privilege to do, we are well aware that our children go forth in this unfriendly and ungodly world to encounter temptations, whose strength neither they nor we can estimate. We know not but that beyond our sight there may be undermining seductions of evil; we know not but that beyond our strength of guardianship there may be pending heavy strokes of calamity; we know not but that when our heads are low in death, there may be found in them a maturity of evil from unhappy passions we have neglected to curb, or from the absence of wholesome restraints, which we have neglected to impose. These are thoughts to make a parent watchful and prayerful and earnest, that in the spring time of early youth he may uproot every evil plant, and sow in his children's hearts the good seed of the kingdom for a harvest of usefulness and glory.

Oh, happy parents of Moses! what a rich increase has ensued from the humble planting of faith and piety, in that lowly habitation by the reedy Nile! "Take this child and nurse it for me, and I will give thee thy wages," said the king's daughter to the yearning mother. But what were wages that would drain the wealth of Pharaoh, compared with the gushing emotions of maternal love, that would have taken and nourished that babe, if allowed to do so, even in the most self-denying circumstances? And what was the luxury of even such parental tenderness, compared with the holy rewards of faith and love and self-denial, which are now enjoyed in heaven by those who prepared for a life of eminent usefulness such a son as Moses! The thoughts of a parent must wisely consider things beyond the tomb. The rewards of parental faithfulness in the world to come, from that God who gives us children to nurse for him, no mortal mind can declare. Next to the agony of losing one's own soul must be the distress of a child's everlasting departure from God; and next to the happiness of knowing that we ourselves are accepted before God, is the blessedness of knowing that our children are the friends and servants of the Lord Jesus Christ.

CHAPTER VII.

MOSES CHOOSING ISRAEL.

"This above all—to (God and self) be true,
And it must follow as the night the day,
Thou canst not then be false to any man."
SHAKESPEARE.

WE have no information of the life of Moses from his childhood until he reached adult years. Doubtless the daughter of Pharaoh, who "nourished him for her own son," took pains to have him educated under the most competent Egyptian teachers, and trained in the manly exercises and warlike arts which belonged, in those ages, to the nurture of a noble youth. The Scriptures say that "Moses was learned in all the wisdom of the Egyptians; and was mighty in words and in deeds:" Acts vii. 22. That is, he was instructed in the civil, political, and military knowledge of that people; and doubtless he learned thoroughly their religious teachings, though he did not adopt them. Josephus declares that he was a leader in the Egyptian armies; and this is quite consistent with the character and conduct elsewhere assigned to him. It is not unlikely that there was a period in the life of Moses when his pious parents were deeply anxious in watching his career. They had carefully trained him to know the Lord God of his fathers; they had intrusted him with the secret of his birth and of his believing preservation; and yet they could not prevent his subsequent exposure to all the temptations of an Egyptian training. But the prayers that had invoked God's delivering mercy when he was laid by the water's brink, were still sent on high; or if, before this, his parents were already dead, their prayers were recorded and remembered before the eternal throne.

We would like to trace, if we could, the array of means which led Moses to forsake Egypt, and cast in his lot with the sons of Jacob. We number first parental instruction and parental prayer. Perhaps also he was influenced by illustrious examples in past ages; especially, perhaps, by one illustrious name, honourably recorded in the annals both of Egypt and of Israel. The sacred writings set before us the example of some eminent believers, who have in the full prime of their powers, and with the prosperous world all before them, deliberately chosen reproach and poverty and self-denial with the people of God. The glory of true piety is its power to surpass all worldly attractions to the mind of a believer. It may be that the mind of Moses was much affected by the example of the patriarch Joseph, who at the age of thirty years had so good an opportunity of grasping the honours and wealth and pleasures of Egypt; but who so nobly kept himself aloof from all that was defiling; kept his early faith in Israel's God; gave full proof, for eighty long years of prosperity, that his heart was with the sons of Jacob; and then transmitted his memory, by a solemn covenant, for the assurance to his people that Egypt was not their home.

But if even we cannot trace the steps of Moses as he turned his back upon Egypt, we can recognize the nature and wisdom of the choice he made; and in nothing concerning Moses have we all a deeper personal interest than in this change. For the essential elements of true piety are the same in all ages; it was true then as it is true now, "Except a man be born again he cannot see the kingdom of God;" and just such a change as Moses met must pass upon each one of us, in order to our acceptance before God. We may not be in like circumstances; but we are partakers of the same nature, we are under the same law, we need the same regenerating grace as Moses.

We are told of Moses, that "when he was come to years, he refused to be called the son of Pharaoh's daughter:" Heb. xi. 24. Whatever impressions may have been made upon him from his earliest years; however changing may have been his purposes and thoughts while yet he was but a child; even though his conversion to God may have taken place early, we are assured that he ratified his choice when an intelligent and mature mind carefully and deliberately considered the entire matter. And there seems no just reason why we should not rank the faith of Moses among the great triumphs of Divine grace, as remarkable, yet as rational, as the change in Saul of Tarsus. We may very easily conceive that the astonishment of the Jews long after this, when Saul, the persecutor, became Paul, the preacher, was no greater than the amazement of the Egyptians, when a young man, trained in their court and accustomed to the luxury of the palace, deliberately stepped forth to take his place among that rude, enslaved people, whose laborious toils were spent by the borders of the Nile. To the minds of the Egyptians there was doubtless something even ungrateful in the stand now taken by this ingenuous young Hebrew. By the care of the princess, his life had been saved; she had nurtured him for her own son: she had caused him to be fully educated; and he had prospects of honour and dignity in the land. She might reasonably expect some returns for this kindness. And doubtless the mind of Moses fully appreciated the position in which he stood, weighed the attractions of the world, and felt similar perplexities to those which have often troubled the anxious and inquiring man. There were not indeed wanting thoughts to vindicate the course which Moses took, even in the eyes of those who might have acted otherwise. If he had been rescued from the water by Pharaoh's daughter, yet it was Egyptian cruelty that had put his life in jeopardy. If he had been trained in ease and luxury, apart from his brethren; yet again it was Egyptian injustice that had reduced those brethren to poverty and toil. He was educated and honoured; but Egyptian tyranny had kept the Israelites in bondage and ignorance. The highest personal respect, therefore, upon the part of Moses towards his benefactress, and the warmest gratitude for her kindness, might still exist when he chose most decidedly to go with the children of Abraham.

And surely a candid Egyptian must have acknowledged that the change in Moses was entirely above all suspicion of dishonourable, or even inferior, motives. The motives which usually actuate unprincipled men, and lead to ungrateful or wicked conduct, could have no power in a case like this; and as for selfish motives, they all manifestly urged him in an opposite direction. Had Moses fulfilled the wishes, and, as men might say, the reasonable expectations of those who had befriended him, ease would have been his lot, rather than toil; pleasure, rather than affliction; riches, rather than poverty; the favour of the king, not his wrath; a place among the rulers, not among the slaves; the delights of learned society, rather than the company of the ignorant. Even hostile and prejudiced minds could not question that the conversion of Moses to the Jewish faith was effected by no power of ambitious or selfish motives. The world seldom presents stronger charms, or binds down the heart of man with stronger ties, than were gathered around this man.

The grace that converted Moses is none the less remarkable because we can see the proofs of Divine favour through all his life ; and its triumph when he turned his back upon Egypt is as excellent as any recorded in the history of the church. The only controlling reason for his decision is found in religion. True principle, the leadings of conscientious conviction, made him refuse the honours of Egypt. He teaches us that no ties of education, of worldly advantage, or even of gratitude for kindness shown, should prevent our just service to God. We need not lose our kindly feelings towards men from whose views and practices we are constrained to stand apart. This man could cherish the memory of Pharaoh's daughter, and yet renounce and abhor the idols and the idol worship to which she was addicted. Perhaps for no other reasons could he be justified in his course. But when a man is influenced by truth and a desire to glorify God, everything not in harmony with these should give way; and any forsaking of worldly plans and associates, any transformation of character and life, may legitimately spring forth from these things. Wisdom, justice, duty, and true kindness to man, ever prompt us, at whatever sacrifices, to yield ourselves to God's service. Nothing is wise or reasonable, if the worship and glory of God are not.

The choice of a religious life does not take the heart of man by storm, in any such sense as to preclude just and deliberate thought. On the contrary, the most thorough awakening, and the most urgent anxiety of a sinful soul, should not interfere with the clearest exercise of wise intelligence.

Moses is an example to all time after him: and in his choice every man may see the principles by which we should all be animated.

CHAPTER VIII.

THE GREAT CHOICE.

"The son of Amram spurns the regal prize,
From pride and luxury the hero flies;
Forsakes the Egyptian court with cheerful zeal,
And pleasure finds and joy, with lowly Israel."

FEW men have ever made choice of religion under more unfavourable circumstances, or at greater sacrifices of an earthly kind, than Moses. He is, for this, only the more excellent example; for we may find among the things he surrendered, and among the things he chose, the recognition of every principle which men must acknowledge in every land and age, when they forsake the world for the church of God. Few men have given up more of the world, or when they were better able to hold it, than Moses did. And when we see how reasonable and excellent his choice was, we have the stronger argument to show that the embrace of the same principles, with all their consequences, is yet more reasonable for other men.

Religion, in his case, is considered as the free choice of a reasonable soul. So it ever is. For the influences of Divine grace, desirable and necessary as they are, do not interfere with the freedom of man's will. Now in every choice there is implied the refusal and the acceptance of certain things; and these things must be considered; and the man, and the motives which influence him, must be considered, that we may justly estimate the choice itself.

We bring before our minds,

I. The World he surrendered.

Substantially the world is the same to every man; all its attractions may be included in a brief summary that is the same in every age; and though the prospects and the possessions of men are as different as possible, men all hasten onward in much the same paths. Three especial things engross the thoughts of men: honour, pleasure, and wealth. All these, and in their brightest forms, were spread before the mind of Moses; and he renounced them all.

The path of honour sometimes leads a man to seek power by ambitious enterprises, or by the influence of superior wisdom and learning. Had Moses been an ambitious man, he had many opportunities to gratify such a passion. Educated in a warlike age, and among a warlike people, we can scarcely doubt that he was bred to arms; and without adopting the opinion of Josephus, that the princess wished to make him the heir of the throne, we may believe that a man of his capacity might have gone forward to a splendid career, had he been ambitious to serve in the Egyptian armies. And the success he afterwards achieved in his writings, plainly shows, that as a man of learning, the prospect of honourable distinction lay before him.

The riches of Egypt are named expressly among the things renounced by Moses. Earthly riches are exceedingly attractive to earthly minds; and not only those who become rich, but those who desire it, fall into many snares and dangerous lusts. And we can well conceive that the surrender of wealth and luxury is a much more difficult thing to one who has from his childhood been accustomed to all their pampering influence. Moses, though the foster-child of the king's daughter, gave up the treasures of Egypt.

The pleasures of sin allured him. And a gifted, noble young man, would find many, in a dissolute, pagan court, to place before him the temptations to the various pleasures which there abound. Nowhere, indeed, would dissolute pleasures be more likely to gain a young man's attention, than in circumstances like those which surrounded this Hebrew lad, at the critical period of his life. But he was willing to surrender the world's enjoyments.

Very inviting indeed must the world have seemed to the eye of Moses. Few men are more capable of excelling in the pursuit of all it offers; few have greater advantages to begin life; few seem more entangled by the circumstances that prevent a man from renouncing the world; and we may therefore conclude that if Moses wisely forsook Egypt, gave up its treasures, and despised its joys, the surrender of a vain world may be justified in any other man.

But we further consider

II. The Church he embraced.

He gave Egypt up for Israel. And there are two special aspects of the church of God which we may notice, as characterizing the choice made by him at this time. We may consider those essential principles of self-denial which always and everywhere belong to piety; and those particular disadvantages of religion that are sometimes greater than at other times, and which are seldom more grievous than as they were borne by Moses. Every man who truly becomes a believer in the gospel must take up his cross. So Paul speaks of him as "suffering affliction with the people of God," and as bearing "the reproach of Christ." Not personal ambition, but the glory of God; not the short-lived, sensual pleasures, which men naturally seek, but the mortification of all these, and the pursuit of joys of a nature wholly different; not earthly riches, but treasures laid up on high, must they prefer, who are truly followers of God, and members of his church. And there is no true piety where a man loves any earthly thing more than Christ, or hesitates at Christ's command to follow him, or refuses in his service to give up property, comfort, or life.

And yet we know that there are prosperous times, when many of the burdens which other ages of the church have borne, do not press so hardly upon the sons of Zion. We may sit under our own vine and fig tree, and have none to molest us. The church of Christ may be honoured in the land, and may embrace among her members the useful and respected of society. And happy is the land where the influence of true religion is largest, and where a consistent profession of piety secures the largest respect. The essential claims of religion, as a system demanding self-denial, purity, and charity, are not changed when the external circumstances of the church are most favourable; but surely it requires far less moral courage to make a profession of religion, at such a time, than in periods of distress and persecution.

But Moses not only gave up the loose principles, and practices, and pleasures, of a heathen land for the strict maxims and stern duties of a holy religion; he embraced this religion at a time when the tide of its unpopularity was at its lowest ebb. Indeed, he passed from one extreme to the other; and embraced the reverse of all he might have kept in the Egyptian court. The high prospects of honour which Egypt offered, he exchanged for the low estate of those downcast brethren who were scattered through the land in bondage and oppression. The pleasures of heathenism he gave up, the treasures of Egypt he renounced—to cast in his lot with the poverty-stricken and the self-denying. As in the case of Paul, so long afterwards, where we can find no trace of selfish or worldly wisdom, dictating his remarkable change, or giving him support in his long and arduous toils, so we may see that Moses gave up everything desirable in the world's esteem for those very things which natural minds wish to shun. And if his choice can be justified, if the worst of religion can wisely be preferred to the best of the world;* then is the example of Moses one of peculiar force, to urge that theirs is the greatest folly who stand back from the service of God, in the happier times in which we live. "The lines have fallen to us in pleasant places, and we have a goodly heritage."

In this change of Moses we consider

III. The Man and his Motives.

It is worthy of our particular notice that, here and elsewhere, the Scriptures bring before us the conversion of men who turn not away from the world because they are unable longer to enjoy it. We see here no death-bed conversion, no change in a man who can hold the world no longer, and who then consents to exchange it for hopes of another. Moses was come to years, that is of maturity, not satiety. With the brightest of the world

* A. Fuller.

before him; he able to judge of it, able to enjoy it; with the pleasures, associates, engagements, and, as many would judge, even the duties of life binding him down; with nothing surely but principle to draw him toward Israel, Moses decided. And God's converting word has no nobler triumphs in any age, and it has just such triumphs in every age; and it is ever a reasonable service when any man yields himself to its influence. When a young man breaks away from the brightest earthly prospects and the strongest earthly ties, and yields himself to God's service, the renewing grace of God is exalted.

But what were the principles by which Moses was actuated; and how can we reasonably justify this great change? The Apostle suggests several terms, which may explain the whole. He says, all this Moses did BY FAITH. And this term implies the reception, on his part, of those great teachings of revealed religion, which had specially been kept among the sons of Abraham, and of which to us, Moses is himself the first authoritative expounder. He had learned from parental lips the Hebrew theology; he had been made acquainted with the covenant made by God with Abraham; he had doubtless compared these teachings with the subtle spirit of the Egyptian idolatry, and he had carefully marked the tendencies of both. And not thoughtlessly, but deliberately, he not only chose the doctrines of Israel, but relied upon the promises of the covenant of God. Israel was now indeed in trouble; had he consulted his own ease; had he been governed by the apparent prospects before him and them; had he not fully believed the word he received, he would still have remained in the court and the pleasures of Egypt.

Three expressions of the Apostle may teach us the characteristics of the faith of Moses. 1st. He "endured as seeing Him who is invisible." He believed the Hebrew doctrine of one living, infinite, omnipresent, unseen God; and conscious of his responsibility to him, desirous of pleasing him, relying upon his promises of support and protection, he acted upon this faith. 2d. He chose "affliction with the people of God" rather than the pleasures of sin; and "the reproach of Christ" before the treasures of Egypt. It is no man's wisdom to choose affliction and reproach for their own sake But Christ and his cause and his people have ever borne reproach; and he is no true follower who is not willing to bear whatever reproach may, in any age or land, attend the consistent profession and support of the principles of the gospel. It seldom occurs that the world cannot promise more to a worldly mind than the gospel promises; but the world promises far more than it ever performs, and its best pleasures are but for a brief season. But Moses did not surrender for nothing all the prospects of honour and gain which the flattering world held forth to attract him. His was no foolish choice, either in itself, or in its prospects. The promise of Christ's coming was, perhaps, a matter of reproach in heathen lips: to receive and rest upon Christ for salvation has ever characterized piety, yet ever been offensive to self-righteous men; true and exemplary piety the world always recognizes, and ever reproaches; the people of God always suffer reproach, and never more than in Egypt; yet, in choosing what the world refused, Moses exhibited the highest wisdom. And the Apostle adds, 3d, That he had respect unto the recompense of the reward. Moses did not expect earthly gains. All earthly prospects he surrendered. He believed, indeed, that Israel should leave Egypt; but we have no reason to judge that his own leadership was before his mind when he cast in his lot with a poor and afflicted people, especially as forty years passed before he truly became their leader. For this life, Moses secured one great blessing, which piety always bestows, and which is, indeed, the highest earthly possession. He gained the approbation of his own conscience. Moses embraced truth and duty; and for every man this is the only proper foundation of true happiness. It is not in the downy couch, the sumptuous feast, the costly apparel, or the sounding honour; but in the approving heart, and in the smile of God, that man can find true peace.

And faith's recompense of reward ends not with this mortal life. Moses was a *believer*. He regarded as living realities the great things promised in the covenant of God; and earth's honours and joys were as transient and fleeting shadows, compared with the substance of his invisible things. What need he care to be called the son of Pharaoh's daughter, who might, by a higher adoption, be ranked among the sons of God? What needed he to care for a perilous crown on earth, whose eye discerned faith's crown of unfading righteousness beyond the sky? What cared he for the pleasures of sin for a season, who was allowed to exchange them for the everlasting pleasures of God's exalted service? Moses made no foolish decision. He has never repented of his choice, and never will.

Perhaps human history nowhere else records so remarkable a renunciation of worldly prospects, as in the case of Moses. Emperors and kings have renounced their thrones and retired to private life; but always through pride or selfishness, and never once at the bidding of righteous principle, while yet in the vigour of their own powers, and in the full tide of honour. Moses stands alone. And if we can see in him every characteristic of a genuine piety, contempt for the world, love towards God's people, faith in God's promises, patience in long trials, and zeal to do the will of God, why should we not place him before us, as an example for our own imitation? Indeed, should we not much more imitate him, since we have, in many things, the advantage of him; clearer instructions in the doctrines and privileges of God's people, happier times and less arduous services invite us to choose the same God, and to walk in the same steps.

CHAPTER IX.

MOSES IN THE DESERT OF MIDIAN

"The good man suffers but to gain
And every virtue springs from pain:
As aromatic plants bestow
But little fragrance as they grow;
But crushed, or trodden to the ground,
Diffuse their spicy odours 'round."

GOLI SMITH.

How long Moses remained in Egypt after the notable change which led him to choose his own people, we cannot decide. But it would appear that already he began to understand his mission as a deliverer. How this call was made known to him, we cannot determine; but we must admit, upon his part, a mistaken conception of the time of success. Neither were the people ready to receive him in this capacity, nor he ready to discharge the duties. God usually calls men into his kingdom of grace, and then gives them some work to do there; but the readiness of the young convert to do something, is often far in advance of his preparation, and of his correct estimate of the difficulties before him. The young zeal of Melanchthon was no match for the strength of the old Adam.

Perhaps, in comparing the early zeal of Moses, when he thought "that his brethren would have understood that God, by his hand, would deliver them," Acts vii. 25, with his shrinking back from this same duty at a later time, Ex. iv. 13, we may find the reason for his exile for forty years in Midian, and the proof that these years had not been spent in vain. The early years spent in Egypt have done much to cultivate the vigour of his mind, and to make him acquainted with the elements of human wisdom. But hitherto he has not had enough of that subjection and retirement, which so help a man to know himself, and fit him to bear the heavy responsibilities of life. The wisdom of Divine Providence is quite unlike the wisdom of man. God does not always accept our services when we are ready to offer them, nor esteem us fit for duty when are anxious to engage in it. We might think that Moses, designed for so great duties in the church of God, was, at forty years, of sufficient maturity; and that the active period of his life should begin at eighty, would seem anything but preferable. But this is the Divine plan for the life of the Jewish Lawgiver.

No disapprobation is expressed upon the sacred pages of the act of Moses in slaying the Egyptian oppressor. It is sufficient, therefore, for us to say that too little is recorded respecting the transaction, to justify any censure upon our part. Yet the deed evidently awakened the displeasure of the king, and sent Moses forth as an exile from Egypt. He took refuge in the land of Midian, and having casually aided the daughters of Jethro, he afterwards took up his abode with him. The Midianites were an Arabian tribe, descended from Abraham by his wife, Keturah: Gen. xxv. 2—4. Doubtless they were of nomadic habits; for though we read that Moses, in keeping the flocks of Jethro, led them to Mount Sinai, we afterwards understand that his father-in-law lived at a considerable distance from the encampment of the Israelites: Ex. xviii. This is again confirmed by the apparent familiarity of Hobab, his brother-in-law, with the region of country through which Moses was to pass: Numb. x. 31. Raguel or Jethro is called a *priest* of the Midianites: this may refer as much to civil as to religious power.* We have no means of deciding how far these descendants of Abraham may have preserved pure the religion of the patriarchs. We have not the slightest evidence that they were idolaters; and as Moses invited his brother-in-law to join himself to Israel, Numb. x. 29—31, and as this invitation seems afterwards to have been accepted, and their descendants dwelt among the people of Israel, Judges i. 16, it is likely that the religion of this portion of the Midianites was free from idolatry, and not much different from that of Moses.

* Sheykh exactly expresses the union of the religious and political influence. Smith's Dict. Bible, ii. 426.

When Moses fled from Egypt, he sat down by a well in the desert. Perhaps he sat there weary and thirsty; and, like another, in later times, he had nothing to draw with, and the well was deep: John iv. 11. Here his valour and warlike skill prevailed to drive off the shepherds, who would have prevented the daughters of Jethro from watering their flocks. At the invitation of their father, he joined himself to the tribe; and, like Jacob with Laban, served him as a master, until he married into the family. We have no record of the date of this marriage. Forty years after his flight from Egypt, his sons are spoken of as being yet children: and the Ethiopian—rather the Cushite—descent of his wife was made a matter of unjust reproach on the part of his kindred. Yet here the term Ethiopian signifies Arabian, not African.

So far as we are able to gather from the narrative, the condition of Moses in Arabia was one of great affliction and humiliation. What an affecting contrast may we draw between the worldly advantages possessed by him in the Egyptian palace, and the menial position of herdsman in those deserts. Even his marriage was humiliating. He was not able, according to the customs of those lands, to pay a dowry for his wife; and perhaps she and her family only despised the folly that could surrender his prospects in Egypt, and regarded him as one dependent on his father-in-law for his daily bread. The names he bestowed upon his sons seem to indicate the changeful feelings of Moses; dejected, yet hopeful; not comfortable in the land of exile, yet not at all disposed to give up his faith in the God of Jacob. He called the first Gershom—"a stranger here," or, as some say, "a desolate stranger;"* but the other Eliezer—"God is my help:"† Ex. xviii. 3. His poverty may be gathered from the manner of his return to Egypt; himself on foot, and one poor beast for his household. Was not Moses disappointed in the advantages to be gained by leaving Egypt for Israel? Not at all. Doubtless, in these long years, there were many hours of darkness. Many a time, it may be, faith drooped in dejection. But thus God was carrying on his work in the heart of Moses; and he was gathering treasures of experience, that made him richer than gold. Divine wisdom carries on its work *in* the man, rather than around him; improves the *hearts* of believers, rather than their *property;* and the humiliation of which his people so largely partake, is a necessary preparation for the exaltation they are yet to share.

And while in one land God is fitting the deliverer of Israel for his work, the people in Egypt are passing through a like process of humiliation; and they are the more dejected, because they know no man at all fitted to project their redemption. If any of them *had* fixed their thoughts upon Moses, they have now lost sight of him for nearly half a

* Bush. † See Kurtz's Hist. Old Cov. i. 196, 197.

century. The oppression still continued; the change of rulers brought no salutary change in their condition; but this beneficial result, at least, came of their anguish—that the people cried unto God. In all times, this is the strength of Zion; and God puts his people upon praying before he rises for their relief. They cried unto him; he remembered his covenant, and the day of deliverance drew near. How instructive is the lesson, and how frequently is it repeated in the teachings of God's word, and in the workings of his providence, that when God's people are driven to their knees to put him in mind of his covenant, the time of relief is near! God arises and has mercy on Zion, and the set time of her favour is come, when her people take pleasure in her stones, and favour her dust: Ps. cii. 13, 14. And it often happens that the mass of the professed people of God are engrossed in worldly cares, and forgetful of him, when a few burdened and humble ones draw near with tearful supplications, to ask God's delivering mercy. In all ages the Lord of Zion has been the hearer of prayer, and no earnest cry from his suffering people is ever unheard by him.

Horeb and Sinai are names used interchangeably in the writings of Moses; yet, distinctively, Horeb is the name applied to the range of Arabian mountains,* and Sinai is a single mountain. Upon one occasion, Moses led his father-in-law's flocks to that

* Robinson's Bib. Res. i. 177, 551.

part of the desert which is in sight of Horeb, perhaps of Sinai, as it is called the mountain of God: Ex. iii. 1. Here he saw a vision. A thorn-bush on the side of the mountain flamed with fire, and yet was not consumed. And as the astonished shepherd drew near to see this strange sight, we too may desire an insight into this great mystery.

But as Moses approached the spot, a voice addressed him, bade him draw not too near, and to put off his shoes from his feet, for he stood on holy ground. Oriental customs differ very much from ours. With them the shoe is a mere sole, worn to protect the foot from injury, not from dust and dirt. So the feet of a guest are washed, among the common hospitalities of the land; so while we uncover the head as a token of reverence, they always keep this covered, and uncover the feet. Visitors entering a dwelling, or scholars a school, put off their shoes. Especially upon entering any sacred place, the shoe must be put off. Christians, Moslems, and Pagans, observe the same custom. So the priests were, after this, commanded to minister before God barefooted. And surely the significancy of this should ever be upon our minds, when we appear in the sanctuary where God manifests himself. The place where we stand is holy ground. We do not see a burning bush, nor tremble before a flaming mountain. We may come with holy boldness. Yet let us ever remember God's presence; let us cultivate godly fear; let us repress irreverent familiarity. Ours is a high and holy privilege, when we approach God through the new and living way, Heb. x. 19; but the more humility and seriousness we possess, in every time of worship, the greater will be both our delight and our profit.

CHAPTER X.

THE BURNING BUSH.

"Do deep afflictions try, like gold,
Thy faith? Then with the prophet turn,
Draw near the mountain side, behold
How unconsumed a bush doth burn!
Put off thy shoes and veil thy face,
For God is in the holy place." ANON.

God's works and wonders are never in vain; design marks every work, and significancy every emblem. Man feigns miracles that have no efficacy, and wonders that have no meaning; but this is the excellence of Divine teachings, that simple terms are often full of expression, and call forth our admiration, that so great things can be taught in so brief a space. And the Scriptures doubtless give us so many emblems and parables, because they are both easily remembered and filled with abundant instruction.

Moses saw *a bush*, a bramble bush; not a stately palm, or a magnificent cedar. This bush is taken as an emblem of Israel, the church of God. A similar figure is used long afterwards, by the prophet Zechariah, i. 8, in whose vision a grove of myrtles in a lowly valley, is made to represent the afflicted church. The contrary figure of a lofty tree to signify a proud and flourishing empire, is used by Ezekiel, xxxi. 3, and Daniel, iv. 10–12, respecting Assyria and Babylon. Glorious as are the things that are spoken of Zion, her fitting similitude, hitherto in the world's history, is the humble bush. Especially when the shepherd prophet stood in the desert of Sinai, this emblem suited Israel. Egypt might then be set forth as the forest tree; but Jacob was overshadowed and lowly. And if not as to condition, yet as to characteristics, so must the church ever be in the world. Not the mighty, but the weak, not the proud, but the humble, are called. God condescends to men of low estate, and the gospel of Christ is preached to the poor.

But the bush was not the remarkable part of the vision. It burned with fire, and was not consumed. This it was that drew the attention of Moses. Two different interpretations have been put upon this emblem. 1st. Many have regarded the fire as emblematic of the afflictions endured by the people of God; and to which Israel, in Egypt, was now subject: and, 2d, Others take it as an emblem of God himself, dwelling in the church; a holy God, yet not consuming a sinful people. Yet there seems no just reason why these interpretations may not be combined. It is true that God dwells in the church; and even the afflictions she is called to bear are under his providence.

In the Scriptures, fire is sometimes an emblem of destruction, and sometimes of purification. The difference sometimes pertains to the qualities of the substance subjected to the action of fire. Wood it will destroy, silver it will refine. But God often appears in fire; as to Moses at the giving of the law; to Isaiah in the temple, vi. 4; to Ezekiel by the river Chebar, i. 4; and Daniel saw a fiery stream flow before him, vii. 10. He led his people in the wilderness by a pillar of fire; the baptism of the Holy Ghost is called a baptism of fire, Matt. iii. 11; and his final coming to judgment shall be revealed in fire. The holiness of God is fitly represented by fire. He purifies his friends as the fire purifies silver; he destroys his foes, as fire consumes hay, wood, and stubble: 1 Cor. iii. 12, 13. The presence of God in the church is as fire, that consumes not the bush, but which yet kindles upon and burns that which touches the burning bush.

And there is a close connection between the indwelling holiness of God, in his church, and in every individual believer, and the persecutions and afflictions which they endure from a hostile world. The holiness of God demands that his people should also become holy; and the means he is pleased to use to secure this end are various. Not by direct but by indirect agencies does God often work in promoting his purposes; and the afflictions and sorrows whereunto his people are appointed, are proof of his holiness as truly as the sanctifying power of his Spirit. The severity of affliction to which the people of God are subjected, is fitly set forth by the emblem of fire. No agent is more searching than fire; no trials are more severe than those to which the church has been exposed. It may give us, on the one hand, a serious idea of those sins and earthly defilements, from which we cannot easily be freed; and, on the other, a profound knowledge of God's love for holiness, that by such costly methods he forms a people fit for his service. Trials of faith in the hot furnace of affliction are much more precious than of gold. The white robes of the redeemed, garments of humility and love and holiness, are worn by those that have come out of great tribulation: Rev. vii. 14.

In Egypt the church burned with fire, yet not without the appointment of the Lord, and not without her "needs be," 1 Pet. i. 6, in the Divine discerning. There were the fires of temptation, as the pomp, and pleasures, and vices of idolatry addressed them; and fires of persecution, as their oppressors laid heavy burdens upon them, and made their lives bitter with hard bondage.

And the fire *burned* them. When we read of the troubles of past days, we are not to think that our brethren, who endured all these trials, were Stoics. They were "men of like passions with ourselves;" as desirous of ease and pleasure, as fearful of pain, as we. When the fellow-sufferer of the Mexican prince, Guatimozin, cried out under the anguish of his tortures, his complaints were silenced by the invincible fortitude of his king: "Thinkest thou that I lie on a bed of roses."* The weary years passed away as slowly, the nights of suffering were as long, the fear of death was as startling, and the pains of the stake were as dreadful, in the experience of the innumerable martyrs of the church, as like things would be now to any of us. Cruel mockings and scourgings, bonds and imprisonment, dishonour and death are none the less severe for human nature to bear, because the grace of God refines that nature. As tender nerves belong to a believer as to any other man; as feeling a heart beats in his bosom; and, if principle permitted, he would as gladly escape trouble, and do as much to avoid shame and suffering, as any other man. Nor does piety relieve us from those natural fears and apprehensions under which its office rather is to sustain us. Doubtless many a time, in view of their long stay in Egypt, and the severity of their oppressors, the sons of Jacob feared that they should never go forth from the land of bondage, nor inherit the promised Canaan. God never meant that his people should be unfeeling in the trials they are called to bear; and the fears of faith are not regarded, in his sight, as the failing of faith. The more we feel and fear, while yet we rely on him and persevere in his service, the more illustrious is faith's triumph.

* Robertson's America, 252.

The bush burned, but did not burn up. The church, in the fiercest fires, suffers, but is not consumed. The Apostle says of himself, that he was "troubled on every side, yet not distressed; perplexed, but not in despair; persecuted, but not forsaken; cast down, but not destroyed:" 2 Cor. iv. 8, 9. How many have been the fierce trials of the church of God in the past ages of her changing and sorrowful history. "Many a time have they afflicted me, may Israel now say, ... yet they have not prevailed against me:" Ps. cxxix. 1, 2. Egypt and Assyria, Babylon and Persia, Rome Pagan and Rome apostate have arrayed themselves against Zion; her sons have been cast into the Nile, scourged by task-masters, scattered abroad to gather stubble for undiminished tasks; they have been exiled from their homes, cast into the burning furnace, exposed to fierce beasts of prey; they have been imprisoned by Cæsar and by Pope, massacred at Rome and at Paris, burned in the imperial gardens, and at infamous Autos-da-fe; and heretics within and infidels without, have sought by every conceivable method to attack the towers, and to undermine the battlements of the city of our God. And we say not that all these things have been in vain. Many a time has the fierce shout of victory gone along the triumphing lines of the foe; and many a time have timid soldiers in the ranks of the sacramental host, felt serious fears that all was lost. But the church is not consumed. She has never even been in real danger of it. Let faith ever triumph over the strongest fears. In the burning bush God dwells, and the humble abode of his holiness is unconsumed.

Nor have the people of God ever been ignorant of the true reason why the church has been unconsumed. As for the sons of Zion, they have often been weak and in perplexity, and apparently without resources. As for her foes, they have often been strong and triumphant, with victory just within their grasp. How near were the calamities of Israel to a disastrous issue, when the little ark of bulrushes was tossed upon the Nile; when the decree of Haman went forth through all the Persian empire; and when the German emperor thundered against the rising Reformation. But the Red Sea song, "The Lord is my strength and my salvation," has not only filled the lips of God's people in the time of an unexpected triumph, but has even tuned their hearts to gladness in the hour of grief and darkness. "It is said of Luther that when he heard any discouraging news, he would say, Come, let us sing the forty-sixth Psalm."* It is a song for trials. "God is our refuge and strength, a very present help in trouble." It explains the safety of Zion. "God is in the midst of her, she shall not be moved." vs. 1, 4. How plainly can we see in this that God's ways and thoughts are not as ours. The slender bush seems

* Henry in loco.

more combustible and more easily destroyed than if it had been a stately cedar. Yet it is not consumed. For many reasons, the kingdoms of this world have more apparent elements of power and durability than the church of God. They have wealth, and gather more around them; they have strong cities, and they fortify themselves with impregnable bulwarks; they have armies, and they go forth to conquer. If ancient Babylon possessed but a tithe of the splendour and power ascribed to her, we need not wonder at the pride and confidence of the great king, who looked around upon the evidences of his majesty, and said, "Is not this Babylon, that I have built?" These earthly kingdoms are mighty; and their sons grow up to gather their warm affections around the thrones and the fame of their fathers. But the church of God is a feeble kingdom, and many a son has risen up to renounce his father's faith, and to prove himself a traitor to his king, and an apostate from his God. Every subject of the kingdom of grace must be renewed from nature; and thus the perpetuity of this kingdom depends upon the conversion of foes to friends. That such an empire as the church of God can stand through so long ages, against so many adverse influences, and with increasing power as time grows older, is the greatest of God's wonders shown to the sons of men. It is manifestly his wonderful working. Such enemies as the church has known; such various attacks of fraud and force and cunning; such malice and pertinacity of opposition; such alliances from opposite quarters, no kingdom ever before withstood. The weakest empire, judging on earthly principles; one that receives, but inflicts not injury; that sheds her own blood, not that of her foes; and that answers the curses of her enemies by invoking blessings upon them, is the most ancient and permanent kingdom in the world. But hers is imparted, not inherent strength. One Friend dwells in Zion, so mighty to save, that her children may ever say, with a prophet of their own, "They that be with us are more than they that be with them," 2 Kings, vi. 16. The plans of all the foes of Zion are known to him; for all their cunning his wisdom is an overmatch; from all their power his single arm can deliver; and the opportune time to interfere he chooses, and the feeblest instrumentality he can make effectual for the most glorious deliverance. Blessed is the church of God! blessed every member! for the bush burning with fire is never consumed; the covenant of God ever stands fast with his people. Happy is the man upon whom comes the blessing long after this pronounced by Moses upon the tribe of Joseph, not only "for the precious things of the earth and the fulness thereof," but "for the good-will of Him who dwelt in the bush," Deut. xxxiii. 16.

He, who appeared to Moses in that burning bush, was the great revealer of the Godhead, known to us, in his incarnate estate, as the Lord Jesus Christ. He is called "the Angel of the Lord;" the Angel-Jehovah in Hebrew; מלאך יהוה; and yet declares "I am the God of thy fathers." This Divine, uncreated Angel, is the messenger of God, in whom was the Divine name. A careful comparison of what is taught us in both the Old and New Testaments, will show that only the Second Person of the adorable Trinity has made known God to man. This the Apostle John expressly affirms, and further proof of it will lie in our way as we pass further on in the life of the Jewish Lawgiver, John i. 18.

In arguing with the Sadducees, who appear to have denied both the resurrection and the connected doctrine of the future life, Acts xxiii. 8: Mark xii. 26, our blessed Lord refers to this scene of the burning bush; corrects their crude ideas respecting the social condition of the pious dead; and argues for the future existence of the patriarchs, from the words here divinely used concerning them. Many years after the death of Abraham, Isaac and Jacob, God says not, I *was* their God, but I *am* their God. The argument is, "they therefore must be living men; if living, it must be as disembodied spirits, for their sepulchres are still with us; yet they are still the patriarchs." This simple refutation of the Sadducean doctrine respecting separate spirits, he regards as drawing with it the overthrow of their error touching the resurrection. The personal existence of the patriarchs involves the res urrection of their bodies.

And it may be added that our Lord's method of arguing implies the most entire confidence upon his part in the exact correctness of the very words of Moses. An argument of the greatest import is made to hinge, not upon a series of statements, or a long narrative, whose drift cannot be mistaken, but upon a simple single statement, that God to Moses declared himself the God of patriarchs, who had already passed from the earth! And, here and elsewhere, the entire influence of our Lord Jesus Christ obviously goes to uphold the Old Testament Scriptures in all their purity, integrity, authority and excellence.

CHAPTER XI.

THE REVEALED WILL OF GOD DESIRABLE.

"Sad error this, to take
The light of nature rather than the light
Of revelation for a guide. As well
Prefer the borrowed light of earth's pale moon,
Or the dim twinkling of a distant star,
To the effulgence of the noonday sun."

THE evident unwillingness of Moses to accept the charge now urged upon him, doubtless sprang from profound views of his own insufficiency. In his younger days, he was ready to take upon him the office of a prophet of God and the deliverer of Israel; but now it is otherwise. His new feelings sprang partly from a better self-acquaintance, acquired in his more mature experience, and partly from that deep awe and reverence that is always inspired in man in the known presence of God. And nothing is more proper than that man should feel insignificant and unworthy before Him, especially when sinful man comes before his sinful fellowmen as a representative of the Most High God, speaking the words of God, and with authority demanding man's obedience. Who is sufficient for this thing? It becomes the wisest and most gifted man to feel his weakness. And yet to go forward, when called even to such a work, is every man's duty. As it is not by his own power or holiness or wisdom that he does or speaks such great things, he may be humble in himself as an instrument, and yet bold in God's service.

And we all have a deep interest in the call of Moses as the prophet of the living God. He lived long ago, indeed, but he speaks to us; and there is an authority in his commission that can never be lost, so long as man shall live upon the earth. That Moses did things and said things chiefly affecting his own generation and his own tribes, may be true enough; he said other things of permanent value. Especially let us notice this; that Moses stands the first, in the order of time, in the succession of inspired prophets, whom God has sent to instruct the sons of men. Even if other prophets were sent before Moses, which indeed is true, yet all we know of them we learn through him. Moses gives to man the first written pages of revelation. Revelation itself dates back to the origin of our race; but alas! twice already, before the days of Moses, had degenerate man nearly lost the knowledge and worship of the true God. This is the true reason why the revelations made through Moses were communicated to but a small portion of the human family. Men did not like to retain God in their knowledge. Men have thought that they could learn of God all they need to know, without any revelation of his will; and even after long and costly experience, there are still men who stand forth and refuse to believe that it is either possible, desirable, or necessary, that God should reveal his will to man. To us, Moses is the first inspired writer, and as he is here first introduced to us, as an authorized prophet of God, it may be well for us to occupy our thoughts upon the commission thus given him. God begins in him that written record of his will, which was not complete until long afterwards, when his own Son appeared in human flesh. Some of the evidences of the divine commission of Moses will be brought forward hereafter. Now we will consider the desirableness and reasonableness of a divine revelation of God to man; from which, in the next chapter, we will pass to speak of things which prove its necessity.

That a revelation from God to man is impossible, no reasoning of ours is competent to decide. Creatures who are incapable of comprehending the infinite God, are not able to decide what he can or cannot do. Rather, if he desires our worship, it is natural to think that he will instruct us sufficiently for intelligent worship.

And from the nature of man and the importance of the relations we sustain to God, such teachings from God are exceedingly desirable. Our condition in life makes us all dependent; and it is impossible for man to rise above the *influence*, we may even say the guidance of other minds. Look at man in the earliest stages of his being. Why is he so long in reaching that maturity of mind and body that can measurably free him from a helpless dependence? No earthly being is more dependent, or longer dependent than man. No creature needs instruction more, or is so much influenced by it. Hence every child places an almost unbounded confidence in the teachings of others, and, in the early periods of life, we receive our ideas less from reflection than from instruction. To leave a child to himself to form his own ideas, untaught by the wisdom of others, is to allow him to grow up ignorant and uncultivated.

Men are usually what their education makes them. The child of a Pagan becomes a heathen; the child of a Mahommedan becomes a Moslem; and infidel pride and false philosophy point to this as the triumphant proof that all religion is a mere matter of training. But the triumph is too soon, and the inference drawn is false. The fact is a proof of the importance of education; but it is a clear disproof of the infidel claim that human reason is a sufficient guide to the worship of God. If education and reason are different things, then men never have been guided by their reason; and indeed, men are ever, for the first twenty years of life, placed in circumstances where they necessarily depend upon others to guide their feeble judgment, and to teach them truth. And those earliest twenty years of life usually exercise a controlling influence, and determine the character of the man. The fair inference therefore is, man needs a guide to teach him the way of right; and if he has a guide at all, let it be a sure and a good one.

Of course every man must use his own faculties in order to live aright, but it does not follow that we must address ourselves to our most important duties in the use of our *unaided* faculties. Let us consider the case of a serious man in the very important social position upon which so much hinges the welfare of human society. Here is a youthful parent, the guardian of a rising family. He has important and serious duties to discharge towards his children. Much of his time is necessarily occupied by busy efforts to make comfortable provision to clothe and feed and educate them. But duty will not allow him to neglect their moral training. And their immortality, if even only possible, much more if likely or certain, increases the parent's responsibility. He is their natural instructor. Guide them he must; for in a soil so fertile as the human heart, the wheat must be scattered by a good hand, or the tares will be broadcast by an evil one; and that which preöccupies is likely to hold the field in perpetuity. Neglect of duty to them is culpable misconduct, and may be irreparable mischief. Now no parent puts too high a value upon the office he holds, or upon the care he should exercise towards his children. They have within them tendencies to evil, he can easily discover, and they are going forward into a world of snares and temptations and corruptions. And a wise parent would much prefer to see any child he has, laid in an early grave, by the most afflicting calamity that can rend with agony a parent's heart, than to see him live as some men live in the world. Every parental heart fears for the influence of the world upon his children, and wishes the strongest influences of education and companionship and moral principles thrown around them.

And yet how little time he has, and how poor qualifications, for the proper discharge of duties upon which so much is dependent! Many a parent may reflect thus with himself: "Am I capable of guiding my immortal children, and can I feel that I have discharged my duty towards them? I see other men apparently well satisfied with the efforts they have made, but I see their defects. Perhaps I am as self-ignorant as they. In my past life, I see many errors; in my present views there may be many more; the sincere inculcating of my sentiments may be the perpetuating of wrong. How can I avoid it? I am incapable of examining every subject thoroughly. I have neither time nor capacity. I am a helpless and miserable being, if every thing done for my children must depend upon my thorough investigation of principles, my accurate and certain knowledge of facts, my acquaintance with the connections and tendency of every influence. If my child takes sick, I know little of diseases, and less of medicines, and I must trust his life to another man's wisdom. If my property is exposed to improper encroachments, and the living of my household is about to be swept away, I must seek the aid of an attorney, who knows more of the law than I do. If I start on a journey, I put my life under the care of men I never saw; and one foolish or wicked act may hurry me from existence. Thus I am on every hand dependent, and every day, and almost every movement of life proves it. But in the far more important matter of religion for myself and children, I am quite as dependent as elsewhere. The most important questions I am wholly incompetent to solve for them or for myself. I need a guide; and in this most important of all matters, give me not a human and erring teacher, but a divine and infallible one. Give me an instructor that shall leave me subject only to the liabilities of error that necessarily attend a finite mind in its best advantages. Allow me to point my children to a guide that never errs. As error tends to grow worse; as the follies of the parent are copied rather than his virtues; give me a volume whose teachings may be safely followed. As for myself, I am weak, and always have been; ignorant, and always expect to be; liable to be imposed upon and surrounded by many disposed to practise deceitful arts upon me. Surely for me and for my household, and for every man, a volume of Divine Revelation to guide me to the knowledge of truth and God, is exceedingly desirable."

CHAPTER XII.

A REVELATION NECESSARY.

"Revealed religion first informed thy sight,
And Reason clearly sees what Faith unfolds:
'Tis Revelation, what thou thinkest *discourse*,
Else why so clear these truths before thy mind,
To heathen sages hidden or obscure?"

IT seems a very strange thing that man should need any proof that a revelation of God's will to us is desirable or necessary. Yet so great is the estrangement of our corrupt nature from God, that the accumulated evidences of ages are overlooked, and men of our times grope after God as blindly and as vainly in Christian lands, as ever did the heathen in lands of darkness. Surely we can explain this mystery only by the Apostle's solution, given so long since, "They do not like to retain God in their knowledge." Rom. i. 28. When we see men in Christian lands, scorning the light of God's holy word, and eagerly pursuing the *ignes fatuos* that are ever rising and ever disappearing in the corrupt marshes around us; when we see, also, that corruption and licentiousness are the almost invariable characteristics of these things, it seems full proof that not reason, but depravity of heart, is the ruling power to lead these men so far astray. The short-lived existence and the miserable tendencies of these human devices to supplant the simple religion of the Scriptures, ought to warn every man of the flattering deceits by which so many men have been deluded.

Yet it must be acknowledged that in a Christian land the errors of men are incorporated with so many borrowed or stolen truths, and wear such forms of plausible deceit, that the simplest proofs of man's ignorance, uninstructed of God, are not so apparent. Our ideas are necessarily coloured by our circumstances. No man can be educated in all the views and thoughts and practices of a civilized community, and then, by any exercise of the mind or will, transfer himself to the state of a savage. He may go and live, if a depraved taste so inclines him, among barbarous tribes, and adopt their ways and habits; but he must know things they do not, and he must have powers of thought, which, perhaps, he cannot attribute to any special teacher, but which he never would have possessed, had his early training been among the savages. Take an intelligent man from the United States, who never learned a single branch of mechanical business, and who among us would make a miserable mechanic, place him in the heart of Africa, and surround him by a horde of barbarians: he would know far more of what human skill could do, and have a better idea of the methods of working to secure the happiest results of human skill, than any man among them. For ideas are like seeds, they are scattered by every means. Some are planted by human hands, and with great care; some are dropped without special design; some are furnished with light wings, to be wafted by the winds. And, like seeds, these thoughts spring up unobserved; we cannot trace their origin or growth; and favouring circumstances only are needed to bring forth mature fruit from seeds that have been cast into the soil, we know not when or how. And as no man can possibly be a barbarian, who was born and trained among a civilized people, so no man can be a heathen in religious knowledge, who has all his life held intercourse, however slight and casual, with Christians. Even the infidelity of Christian lands owes much to the Bible; and this not only beyond the acknowledgments, but beyond the thoughts of its votaries. Men steal light from the Bible to prove that they do not need the Bible.

The clearest proof that man needs a revelation from God should be shown from the actual history of man as he has lived without one. After twice making known his will to the human race,—first through Adam and then through Noah,—the Supreme Ruler, in wisdom, as the Apostle assures us, 1 Cor. i. 21, resolved to leave men to their own way, to prove by awful experiment, that the unaided wisdom of man could not find out God. When Moses came as a prophet from Jehovah, his mission was specially directed to the Jews, not exclusively, but conservatively, with the ultimate design, expressed repeatedly in his own writings, that all nations of the earth should be blessed, Gen. xii. 3, xviii. 18, xxii. 18, and that the earth should be filled with the knowledge and glory of God, Numb. xiv. 21. If, then, we desire to see how much man needs such teachings, we may look at the nations that for so many ages wandered away from God, and fashioned gods, religion, and morals to themselves after the imaginations of their own hearts.

The dark history of the human race where Moses and the succeeding prophets, in the line where he is first, have not been read, affords serious proof of the need in which men have stood of a revelation from God. Sometimes we hear dolorous complaints from the wise men of Pagan lands, who see enough to know their lamentable ignorance. For Pythagoras declares man's need of divine interposition to teach him his duty.* Cicero confessed that no excellence can exist without celestial inspiration. Hierocles and Seneca tell us that no man can become good without the help of God. Socrates deplored the want of a superior direction;† and Plato admitted that many truths are beyond

* Leland's Deist. Writers, i. 18. † Plato in Alcibiad., II. xii–xxiii. Leland, Ibid. Jamblichus in Vit. Pyth., 28.

the reach of experience, and must be derived from God.* And the entire race testified to the same necessity, even in that very perverseness, which, wandering from the true God, yet received the professed teachings of divinity in false and inferior forms.

But the state of the heathen world of all ages and lands is the proof at once that man needs a revelation, and that the revelation given us in the line of the Jewish prophets, from Moses on Sinai, to John in Patmos, is the divine original. The degrading ideas of Pagan men respecting religion and morals; the myriads of gods they worshipped; the inferior and the debasing characters assigned to these gods; the rites by which they served them; and the history they ascribed to them, are all proofs of their need of a divine instructor. Nor is only the moral character of heathenism to be taken into the account, when we say that by the wickedness of man is the necessity for divine teachings proved. Man, we acknowledge, is wicked in all ages, nations, and places; and beneath the shadow of Christian sanctuaries are dens of dark pollution, and men of gross wickedness, whose deeds of shame may not be mentioned. Yet the moral and social condition of Pagan lands is immeasurably worse than can be found in any Christian land, and especially in one where the Bible is really read. But the most marked and important

* Schools of Ancient Philosophy, pp. 7, 130.

difference between Christian and Pagan lands lies in this, that *there* many crimes are justified and even enjoined, and *here* every crime is in defiance both of law and of public sentiment. In the open day, and glorying in their deeds, the mother has sacrificed her child's life, and the widow her own; the warrior drinks the blood of his fallen foe; the devotee inflicts upon himself agonizing and protracted tortures; and poor human reason is not even capable of throwing off these things as displeasing to God.

Those who dwell among the heathen of modern times, declare solemnly that the pictures so often drawn of ancient morals, are just as true of these communities now. How often has it been repeated that the awful words of Paul, in the close of the first chapter of the Epistle to the Romans, only too truly describe the Pagan world as it yet is. It is not in the power of human wisdom, in its highest forms; it is not within the compass of philosophy or civilization to lift man above the grossest corruption. A few statements of the ancient morals may show us plainly man's need of divine teachings. Livy wrote of Rome, in his times, that morals had so degenerated that "We can neither endure our vices, nor their remedies."* Juvenal is famous for his ridicule of Roman profligacy; and Suetonius could not write the lives of the Emperors without giving such notices of their private charac-

* Livy, Hist. liber i. prefatio.

ters as could scarcely be tolerated in any modern writer. But let us not speak of the common people, or of the profligate rulers. The character of the philosophers and teachers of youth may give us a better idea of the state of morals in ancient Greece and Rome. Quintilian declares that under the name of philosophy the most notorious vices were screened.* Cicero declares that the ancient philosophers never reformed either themselves or their disciples; and that he knew not a single instance in which the teacher or the disciple was made virtuous by their principles. Lucian declares that as a body they were tyrants, adulterers, and corrupters of youth.† If we take up these philosophers by name, the case is not altered. Seneca is regarded as one of the purest moralists of Rome, and wrote thus: "Vice no longer conceals itself; it stalks abroad before all eyes. So public is profligacy . . that innocence has wholly ceased to exist."‡ Yet Seneca was the teacher of the infamous Nero, became the tool of his vices, and publicly apologized for the act of that tyrant in murdering his mother. Diogenes and Crates were unblushing in their lewdness; and more than this might be charged on Aristippus, Xenophon, and many other eminent philosophers. Cicero taught that lewdness was a crime of small magnitude, and Plato and Zeno justified it, the latter adding the

* Instit. Orat. Proem., § 15. † Dwight's Sermons, i. 330.

‡ De Ira, ii. § 8.

doctrine that all crimes are equal.* Seneca† and Pliny‡ argued in favour of suicide, and many eminent men gave it the sanction of their own example. Many of their moralists taught that lying was often profitable; and the murder of their own offspring was regulated by the laws of Romulus, and approved as a prevalent practice by Plutarch and Seneca.§

But let us say no more of the state of morals in these ages and lands, though what has just been said is but an inadequate representation of what the human race has been in all lands and ages, without the revealed will of God. Let us notice some of their crude ideas respecting religion and its special teachings. And when we find them knowing nothing of the true God, or of their own dignity as called to his service, we can scarcely wonder at their wide wanderings into theoretical and practical immorality.

Of God they *knew* nothing. In their conjectures they sometimes made remarkable expressions; like that which Paul quotes from a heathen poet: "We are also his offspring." But Paul's inference that God's offspring should not liken their Maker to wood or brass or stone, the poet never drew. Even if some of the Greek philosophers travelled into Judea, and there gained some knowledge of the teachings of Moses, the ideas thus gained had

* Dwight's Sermons, i. 333. † De Ira, iii. c. 15.

‡ Quoted M'Cosh's Div. Gov. 68. § Horne's Introd. i. 19.

no further influence than to give turn to a few expressions, that have excited surprise and secured attention, like a grain of gold in a clod of clay, from their superior excellence to all else they knew. "According to Themistius there were more than three hundred sects of the western philosophers, differing greatly on subjects of high importance. According to Varro there were two hundred and eighty-eight different opinions entertained by them, concerning the *summum bonum*, or chief good; and three hundred opinions concerning God, or, as Varro himself declares, three hundred Jupiters, or supreme deities. Critias, Theodotus, Diagoras, the Pyrrhonists, New Academics and Epicureans, were generally either Skeptics or Atheists."* That God was fire, or water, or matter, or the soul of the world, were among their various beliefs.† Aristotle questioned the creation of the world;‡ Democritus thought the universe was formed by a fortuitous concourse of atoms; and a like opinion characterized the Epicureans. The immortality of the soul of man was not reckoned among the principles of the Stoics. Aristotle and the Peripatetic school seem not to have believed it. Plato and Cicero argued for it, but with such wavering thoughts that Seneca says that "immortality, however desirable, was rather *prom-*

* Dwight's Serm. i. 319. † Cudworth.

‡ See the Summary in Cicero's Tusc. Quest. Lib., i. chs. ix—xi.

ised than proved by these great men."* How lamentable seem the words of Cicero, after giving the thoughts of many philosophers: "Which of these is true, God alone knows; and which is most probable, is a great question."† How much more deplorable seem the dying words of Socrates to his friends: "I am going out of the world, and you are to continue in it; but which of us has the better part, is unknown to all, except to God."‡

But what was the condition of that part of the heathen world in which Moses had his education? Could he have been furnished in Egypt with any of those remarkable thoughts which have given him his reputation as a prophet of the only true God? It has been alleged by some that many Mosaic laws can be recognized as previously existing among the Egyptian people. If even this is true to a much larger extent than can be shown, it would not be derogatory to his claims as a prophet. We need not believe that the Egyptians had no remains whatever of the true religion, as Noah gave it to all his sons; and if Moses embodied in his laws and teachings every fragment of truth, the proof of his commission would lie in the unerring discernment that gathered the pure and rejected

* Seneca Ep. 102. See also 117.

† Cicero's Tusc. Ques., Lib. i. c. xi. § 23. But see De Amic., c. ii., and De Senectut., c. xxi.

‡ Plato Apologia Socr., xxxiii., in fine.

the vile. Surely the resemblances to Egyptian worship that may be gathered from the teachings of the Jewish lawgiver, are far less striking and important than the contrasts that are palpable. Ancient and modern writers have earnestly contended that Greece received her religion from Egypt.* We know that the Egyptian worship was so debased as to call forth the ridicule of the Romans; and of all these degrading things, Moses has not copied one. The Israelitish people were constantly prone to copy their idolatry; but Moses and their early and later prophets protest against this as constantly.

It is said that the ancient Egyptians knew that God was one. But certainly they did not mean one as Moses taught, to the exclusion of religious honour to any other. The Egyptians worshipped the bull Apis, the crocodile, the ibis, serpents, and other animals, and the leeks and onions of their gardens. So the Roman satirist declares that among them "whole towns worshipped a dog; it was a sin to sink your teeth into an onion; and every garden was overrun with gods."† When a dog died the whole household fasted and went into mourning; and not even the authority of their

*Warburton Div. Leg. Moses, ii. 260. See also the Ægyptiaca of Witsius. For it should be borne in mind that some of the most profound investigators of theological questions, make the Hebrew teachings the sources of even the elder Pagan ideas. See Shedd's Chn. Doctr., i. 205 and notes.

† Juvenal, Sat. xv. 8–12.

Roman conquerors was able to save the life of a soldier who had accidentally killed a cat.

But let us not enlarge on these statements. If on the one hand the dark picture of human ignorance, superstition, and vice, shows man's need of divine teachings, so, on the other hand, the excellence of the things taught by Moses, and by the entire line of Jewish teachers succeeding him, gives proof that the wisdom by which he spoke was not of man. Nor is it any plea against his divine authority that his teachings were not received by his own people according to their real value. For, in one sense, this only shows, with the greater clearness, the excellency of Moses, that he rose so eminent above his own age and people. And it is plain that all divine instructions are so given to man as to give full room for the exercise of free moral agency. Let the teachings and advantages of men be what they may, if they do not like to retain God in their knowledge, he may give them up to believe the grossest falsehoods: Rom. i. 21, seq.

And for this reason it is that we may review the necessities of men for a revelation from God, as these appear in the fearful experiment that for so many ages left the nations to wander in darkness. There is as little danger that in our land and generation the evils of Paganism should come in upon us, as that the praises sometimes bestowed by vain philosophy upon a savage life, should turn us all into barbarians. But when we do not know how much we owe to the revealed truth of God, we do not appreciate it. And many now are willing to cull out some of the teachings of the Scriptures, who yet refuse to take them as the guide in piety and duty. The corruptions of our times are more plausible in their advances, and make high professions of superior knowledge; but they are as really a departure from God as ever were idolatry and Paganism. Thus we may easily know that man needs a guide AS MAN, without regard to his rank, age, times, or learning. "The world by wisdom knew not God," and the most gifted intellects of the world have been fools in the most important, and, as revealed, the plainest of all subjects. Think of modern spiritualism ranking among its votaries some of the strong minds of an age like this, and they, still blinded, though its manifest and growing tendencies are to faith in the grossest absurdities, leading on to the practice of the most vile and polluting abominations! In our own age, and surrounded by the light of our own civilization, there are no greater fools in religion than those who claim to be the wise men of earth; and deism, rationalism, pantheism, materialism, and skepticism have, within the past century, succeeded each other so rapidly, have each made so high claims, to be ridiculed by their respective successors, have shown for how brief a time, and in how narrow a sphere the wisdom of man can make a falsehood current, and have so proved but the gropings of human blindness; that they demonstrate this much, if nothing more, man needs a guide to lead him to his God.

CHAPTER XIII.

ARE MIRACLES CREDIBLE?

"What less than miracles from God can flow?
Admit a God—that mystery Supreme!
That cause uncaused! all other wonders cease;
Nothing is marvellous for Him to do;
Deny him—all is mystery besides." YOUNG.

THAT Aaron is sent forth to meet his brother, and to welcome his return to Egypt, seems to prove two things. 1st. That the brothers were well acquainted with each other. It is likely that Moses, from his childhood, up to the period of his leaving Egypt, had been familiar in his father's house. The Egyptians would regard this but as affection for his nurse, while he himself would understand his true relation to this humble family. There may also have been a measure of intercourse between them during the forty intervening years. The opportunities of the age were imperfect, but still they may have kept up some knowledge of each other. And, 2d. That, simultaneously with the call of Moses, in Midian, to be the deliverer of his people, there was a movement among the Israelites to cry unto God. The people sighed and cried, and their cry came up to God. Ex. ii. 23. And it was in token of their approaching redemption that Aaron received a divine commandment to go forth and meet his brother. Ex. iv. 27

The mission of these two brothers to Egypt was eminently a mission of faith. Two aged men, both far past man's allotted three-score years and ten, came into the dominions of earth's greatest and haughtiest monarch, to demand the freedom of a nation of bondmen. They supported their demand neither by banner nor army, but with the simple waving of a shepherd's wand. And Moses, the chief messenger, is himself obnoxious to Egyptian law, if any now remember the man who fled from the country forty years before.

But they are safe who go upon the Lord's errands. And as Moses now has an extraordinary commission; not simply to deliver Israel, but to speak JEHOVAH'S WORDS in JEHOVAH'S NAME; and as his teachings were to remain of permanent authority, and were to exert an unbounded influence upon all the future character and history of the church of God, so we find him exhibiting testimonials extraordinary, to authenticate his divine commission.

The mission of Moses is the first, in the history of the church, sealed by the power of working miracles. Neither Adam, nor Enoch, nor Noah, nor Abraham, were workers of miracles. As, therefore, these proofs of divine authority hold so important a place in supporting the authority of the Bible; and as the enemies of revelation, with the unerring logic of a native antipathy to divine truth, have made their chief assaults upon this species of evidence, it seems proper that their first appearance in the history of the church should give us occasion to vindicate our faith in these occurrences.

And we may speak,

I. Of the design of the Scriptural Miracles.*

There are two classes of miracles spoken of in the Bible, between which there are three especial points of distinction. They differ in mode, in design, and in times. The first class is composed of such as are wrought by Almighty God himself; sometimes prëannounced to man, but never wrought by man. Such stupendous miracles as the translation of Enoch, the deluge, the confusion of tongues, and the divine (*Theophanies*) appearances to the patriarchs, which were wrought before the days of Moses; and as the wonders recorded in the histories of Jonah, Isaiah, and Daniel, should be ranked among the things which God has wrought. The design of these wonders seems to be to exhibit the personal care of God over the works of his hands. The universe is not a vast mechanism, left to the blind operation of *natural laws*, without the constant care of the Creator. As the object of this class of miracles is to show the providential government of God, so by events proving his rule in

* Of course, on this subject, Trench has become a standard author.

all ages, God hath not left himself without witness. At some times he has borne testimony by such miracles; at other times, by providential workings in human affairs, quite as wonderful as any miracles; quite as good proof of his kindness and wisdom; and quite as truly leading candid men to say, "This is the finger of God."

It is not of this class of miracles that we speak when we say that Moses was the first worker of miracles. We speak of miracles wrought by an intervening human agency. We shall afterwards show that these are not of frequent occurrence among men. Their occurrence is limited by their definite design. Their design is to authenticate the divine commission of a messenger from God. When God sends a man upon an extraordinary errand, to communicate his will to his fellow-men, he furnishes him with extraordinary credentials of authority.

We may now remark,

II. Upon the reasonableness of expecting that such Miracles should be wrought as the proofs of such a Commission.

We may confess that we have no sympathy with those who esteem it strange for God to confirm the claims of his messengers by conferring such miraculous gifts. With the great master of modern philosophy, we are ready to believe almost anything, rather than that this universe has no moral Ruler.*

* Works of Lord Bacon, i. 24, Essay xvi.

Perhaps the very feeling which prompted Bacon to such an utterance, may have given so great currency to fables, in lands and times where nothing better was known. We esteem it highly desirable that God should reveal his will to man; and all needful means to this end are reasonable, for the sake of so great a result. So far from esteeming miracles naturally incredible, we should rather expect to see them wrought, when a just occasion demands.

"Now, in what way," asks Archdeacon Paley, "can a revelation be made, but by miracles?"* And he replies, "In none which we are able to conceive." The revelation of the invisible God in any form must involve a miracle. If he speaks directly from heaven, this is supernatural; if he speaks by any man's instrumentality, that man must afford to his fellow-men sufficient proof to vindicate their faith in so great a claim. The simplest and most unexceptionable proof is the ability to do that which divine power alone can accomplish. So Moses says, "Behold, they will not believe me, nor hearken to my voice; for they will say, the Lord hath not appeared unto thee." Ex. iv. 1. Therefore, when he was sent, the charge to him was: "See that thou do all those wonders before Pharaoh, which I have put in thine hand." Ex. iv. 21.

Nor is there any just reason to say that the

* Evidences of Christianity Preparatory Considerations.

exercise of extraordinary and special powers is any interference with the otherwise uniform and unchangeable "order of nature." The moment we assign a special place to miracles, and a special intelligent design for their occurrence, we confirm and establish the ordinary law. This is just the meaning of the well established formula, *Exceptio probat regulam.* The exception establishes the rule. Indeed, miracles would either be impossible, or they would be without force to attest a revelation, if such phenomena occurred casually, i. e. if the *ordinary course of providential law was not* INVARIABLE. As we cannot gainsay the divine power to work miracles, nor question the efficiency of such testimony to authenticate the divine commission of any prophet; as an object so important will fully justify such displays of divine agency, nothing more can be reasonably demanded than that the miracles wrought should in all things accord with their professed design to honour and glorify God. In the nature of the miracles themselves; in the nature and clearness of the proof that substantiates them; in the comparative rareness of their occurrence in the history of the world; and in the influence, then and ever since, exerted by them, we may see just reason for crediting the divine authority of that Sacred Volume to which God himself has borne witness "with signs, and wonders, and divers miracles, and gifts of the Holy Ghost, according to his own will." Heb. ii. 4. The points thus briefly suggested will be noticed more fully in the succeeding chapter.

It is a remark well worthy of notice,

III. That the Religion of the Bible alone professes to be based upon the miraculous evidences of a Divine commission in its Prophets.

It may suit the enemies of all religion to refer all miracles, true or false, to one class; but truth requires that an important distinction be made between the Scriptural miracles and all others. Other religions claim that miracles have been wrought in their support; and many false claims have been set up in behalf of corrupted forms of Christianity. But this is true, especially of Moses and of Jesus Christ, that their miracles were wrought as the foundation of the people's confidence in them. Moses stood before the Israelites, who had not seen him for nearly half a century, and before the hostile Egyptians, and wrought these wonders of great power. Christ stood before a generation that crucified him, and openly said: "If I do not the works of my Father, believe me not." John x. 37. Very different from this is the claim to miraculous powers elsewhere made.

We cannot account for the rise of Christianity at all, without reckoning that its foundation was in miracles. Even the infidel historian, as we shall again notice, must assign *a reputation for working miracles* among the causes for the spread of the gospel. As if a reputation founded upon imposture could be of any possible avail in the beginning of such an enterprise!

The Mohammedan doctors assign to their prophet numerous miracles; some say a thousand, others more than four thousand.* But no claim was set up for any such powers in the prophet until long after his death; and he himself makes no such claims in the Koran. Mr. Paley says he reckoned thirteen distinct places in the Koran where Mohammed speaks of unbelievers demanding signs from him; and in neither of these does he allege that he wrought a miracle in reply to the demand.†

In the church of Rome various claims have been made; but all alike destitute of a historical foundation. The Jesuits allege that their founder, Ignatus Loyola, wrought many miracles; more, indeed, and more numerous, than those of Christ himself. They declare that proof of more than two hundred was laid before the Pope to secure his canonization. He expelled demons—not by a word, but by a letter. He walked many times in the air. He lighted up dark rooms with his shining countenance and glistening garments. But though Loyola lived in an active and intelligent age, no such claims were set up until long after his death. His life was written by his scholar and companion, Ribadeneira, and published in 1572, fifteen years after his death. A new and greatly enlarged edition, with other facts from persons intimately familiar

* Ockley's Hist. Saracens, 66. † Evidence, Pt. II. Ch. ix. § 3.

with him, appeared in 1587: still a different memoir from the Jesuit, Maffei, was published in 1585: yet in neither of these publications is a single miracle ascribed to him. On the contrary, these, his own intimate friends, assign reasons to explain why it did not please God to work miracles by so eminent a servant.

Like things may be said of the Jesuit, Francis Xavier. Though many miracles are ascribed to him, his own published letters make no claim that he wrought any. The apologist of the Romish church can appeal but to a single ambiguous word to support the claim.* Yet it is not improbable that Xavier, labouring as a missionary in distant lands, may have practised upon the credulity of the heathen, by arts which he carefully omitted to mention in his European correspondence. Between all miracles thus alleged, without any attestation from eye-witnesses, or even any mention from cotemporaries; and the miracles recorded in the sacred writings, there is a manifest distinction. It is one thing to declare that a man already famous, had wrought wonders: it is quite another that miracles should lay the foundation for influence and authority.

It is important to keep in mind

IV. That the evidences of the Scriptures are historical, eminently and peculiarly; and all fair attacks upon them should be made by historical deductions.

Scarcely anything is more remarkable in regard

* Milner's End of Controversy, 186.

to these records, as compared with other religious teachings, than their clear and confident appeals to history. Christianity—the religion of the Bible—"alone of all religions, claims to be founded, not on fancy or feeling, but on fact and truth."*

Yet it may truly be said that no assailant of the Scriptural miracles has ever proceeded against them on the method of historical deduction. It is indeed worthy of careful notice that two of the most erudite writers of history in the English language within the past hundred years, were both infidels; have both attacked the evidences of Christianity; and both declined to make their assaults in the very sphere where their competency is acknowledged. When we find men like Hume and Gibbon, neglecting those plain matters of fact, with which as historians they should be conversant; and attacking plain history by the misty aid of metaphysics; not venturing as historians to assert that these things were not so; but claiming as philosophers that they could not be so: their very silence betrays their own convictions that, *historically*, the religion of the Scriptures is unassailable. So Mr. Gibbon says, "The prudent historian will refuse to examine the *propriety*, till he has ascertained the *truth*" of any matter.† Yet both he and

* Rawlinson's Hist. Ev., 233. Sinai and Palestine, 155.

† Dec. and Fall, ii. 349.

Mr. Hume argue principles, and decline to bring forward facts. Surely when professed and hostile historians shrink from any counter-statement upon historical grounds, the friends of a historical religion may be allowed to triumph!

In every age a hundred men can reason profoundly to detect false reasonings, where one is able to make historical investigations. That these men have unwillingly borne testimony just where the truth needed unexceptionable witnesses, enables thoughtful minds, even among the uneducated, to meet and refute their sophistries. Nothing can be done where they have failed. The historical foundation of the Scriptures, with the miraculous claims that cannot be separated from them, stands fast. If the facts could have been contradicted these men would have been forward to do this. They were too shrewd to reason upon statements, where they dare venture a flat denial. We know when Christianity arose and where; by what agencies; against what oppositions; with what peculiar teachings; and attended by what glorious results. Every minor claim is linked to these indisputable truths, so that Moses cannot be false if Christ is true: and Christ cannot be false if the world has any truths worthy of our faith.

CHAPTER XIV.

CHARACTERISTICS OF SCRIPTURAL MIRACLES.

"What most surprises on the sacred page,
Or full as strange, or stranger, must be true;
Faith is not reason's labour, but repose."

YOUNG.

A TRUE miracle should be able to abide every just test that can be applied to it. We desire in this chapter to suggest a few things in which the miracles recorded in the Scriptures seem superior to the wonders that are sometimes alleged as proofs that other religions are on a level with the religion of the Bible. Truth never assumes the garb of falsehood; yet falsehood often tries to pass off for truth.

I. The Miracles recorded in the Sacred Volume are in their own nature such as we might expect to see wrought by the power of a wise and gracious God.

A counterfeit bank-note may profess the same with the genuine, and may imitate it more or less closely. But competent judges can often detect, in the very execution of the work, the hand of an imitator. So the contrast may strike the most casual observer, when we compare the very character of the wonders recorded elsewhere than in the Bible, with the miraculous deeds chiefly herein written. As the sacred Scriptures are remarkable for their freedom from the gross errors that abound in every other ancient book, whether profane or professedly sacred; so the miracles of the Bible stand in a class by themselves, and as compared with others, shine with a lustre peculiarly their own. They are neither charms, nor prodigies, nor monsters, but miracles. Let us lay aside the alleged evidences, and spend a few thoughts upon the miracles themselves. The Mohammedans tell us that their prophet caused the moon to pass through the sleeve of his robe, to separate into two parts, and to ascend up as it was before; that gravel sang in his hand; that poisoned meat spoke and warned him not to eat of it; and that cooked and half-eaten fowls were endowed with life and speech.* The Apocryphal books that pretend to record the early miracles of Jesus, affirm that he miraculously corrected the defects in the workmanship of Joseph as a carpenter; formed images of clay and endowed them with motion and life; in childish petulance revenged himself by striking his playmates dead; and upon the breaking of his pitcher, carried water home to his mother in his cloak.† Among the works ascribed to Simon Magus, we hear of walk-

* Ockley's Hist. Saracens, 66.

† Gospel of the Infancy. Apoc. N. T.

ing statues, brass dogs that barked, and transformations of men into animals.* Among the miracles of the church of Rome, we read of persons conversing for hours and days after their heads were cut off;† of a missionary crossing a river every day for a year upon his hands and knees upon a frozen beam;‡ of a statue inclining its head, and extending its arm to embrace a criminal;§ of a dead body decayed till only the bones were left, asking to make confession;‖ of flowers springing up with the praises of the Virgin Mary written in letters of gold upon the leaves;¶ all these are written in one single volume; and in our own land and times, published with the approbation of their highest dignitary among us. And like things are abundantly written in their traditions. The winking Madonnas, the bleeding images, and the miracle of the blood of St. Januarius, as set forth for the belief of our own age, are familiar to every intelligent person. But all these are as different as possible from the miracles recorded in the sacred volume. When we turn our eyes upon them, we seem to be comparing a coarse clumsy counterfeit bill with the neat and graceful engraving which the hand of a master workman has put upon the genuine note. These wonders are usually as frivolous in their own

* Trench on Miracles, 31. † Glories of Mary, 273, 689.

‡ Glories of Mary published in 1852 with the approbation of Archb'p. Hughes, p. 52. § Pp. 213, 233. ‖ P. 262. ¶ Pp. 692, 693.

nature, as they are vague in the usual purposes assigned to them.

Now in palpable contrast with all these, the Scriptural miracles are appropriate to their place; dignified; in harmony with the character of God; supernatural, but not monstrous; and thus in the very narration of them, having an air of verity which is far absent from these trifling legends.

II. The nature and clearness of the proofs which attest the Scriptural Miracles may distinguish them from all others.

The miracles of Moses and of Christ were such that there was no possibility of mistake on the part of the witnesses. They were wrought in things where every man, ignorant or learned, was a competent judge; openly and before great multitudes of men, some of whom from foes became friends, and others remained foes, yet without venturing to deny these wonders. That historic evidence should be thought complete which infidels have assaulted for sixteen centuries, and yet have never ventured to attack by historic deductions. It is tame to say that no portion of human history is so well authenticated. Such a vast accumulation of historic proof, in original documents, in remaining institutions, in concurrent voices of various writers, in explicit teachings incapable of refutation; such an amount of vigorous inquiry—and from every motive that can actuate man—as have gathered around this single volume, the Bible, does not belong to all the other remains of human history put together. The very fact that the Bible maintains its hold upon the faith and love of man; rather we should say the fact that the Bible is more widely circulated and more zealously obeyed than ever; and this too in the most intelligent communities on earth, and by the most upright and benevolent men the world possesses, seems entirely inconsistent with even the possibility that its claims are falsely founded. No history but a true one, could abide the investigations through which this book has passed. Opposite to this thought is the reflection, that one fact proves the obvious falsehood of infidelity—its grounds of attack are changed with every succeeding age; and we have thus proof that the enemies of the Scriptures are not satisfied with each other's arguments.

III. The object kept in view in the Miracles recorded in the Scriptures is one worthy of the Divine power.

No instance can be shown in which the evident influence of the miracle is not the honour of God. Both those who wrought and those who witnessed the miracles of the Scriptures, ascribe the glory to him. Nicodemus said, "No man can do these miracles except God be with him." John iii. 2. The baffled magicians of Egypt say "This is the finger of God." Ex. viii. 19. The Apostles deny expressly that they did these things by their "own power or holiness." Acts iii. 12. This is just what we should expect, if these are wonders wrought by God to attest the mission of his prophets. And it is a sufficient refutation of the charge that miracles tend to impugn the established order of nature, that no men have more honoured God's providential rule or obeyed the dictates of his law than those who have most firmly believed the supernatural things of the Bible.

IV. The comparative rareness with which these wonders occur in the history of the Church of God is a remarkable testimony to their truthfulness.

And this remark should have the more force, because it is a common impression that miraculous wonders belong to the entire history of the Scriptures, and because the Romish church lays claim to the exercise of miraculous powers, as one of the proofs, to the present hour, of her truthfulness as a church.* This involves a great error in understanding God's ways of dealing with his people. Miraculous powers were rarely granted to the prophets of the Old Testament church: we have no reason to judge that they were to be differently afforded in the New Dispensation.

We have already spoken of two classes of miracles wrought by Divine power; distinct in working, in design, and in the times of their occurrence. The miracles wrought by God himself without human agency, must be carefully distinguished from those wrought through the agency of man.

* Bellarmine's Eleventh Mark.

The definite design of this latter class is to attest the commission of those whom God has sent upon an extraordinary prophetical mission. Miracles of this class are not scattered through all the history of the church: they appear when some new great work is to be done for God; and they cease as soon as the work is fairly established.

So miracles of this class can be found chiefly in three periods of the church. The first period is the age of Moses. It was fitting that the first inspired writer, and the first lawgiver of the church of God should confirm his extraordinary commission by signs from heaven. The second period is the age of Elijah. He was the great reformer of Old Testament defection, almost to apostasy; and the propriety that he should work miracles is less distinct, but similar to that of Moses. The third period, greatest of all in every respect, is that of our Lord Jesus Christ. His were greater teachings and higher claims than the world has otherwise known; and there seems eminent propriety that the Son of God should prove the truth of his claims upon Divinity itself, by stupendous, abundant, and benevolent miracles.

So far from believing that miracles wrought through human instrumentality belong to all the history of God's people, or that the power to work such is a permanent "mark" of the church, we gather from the Scriptures that only an extraordinary mission may appropriately exhibit such testimonials from heaven. The miracles of the Bible of this class, are rare, except as associated with these three names, or as wrought by their immediate successors. It strengthens the proof of genuineness in these great things, that in the three great periods of miraculous wonders, they were not strictly confined to a single person; but as all of them left the earth with their respective labours incomplete, so the immediate successors of each, whose place it was to prosecute the same extraordinary work, were endowed with like powers. If Joshua is to take up the unfinished labours of Moses and lead the people to Canaan, Joshua also works stupendous miracles. If Elisha was to carry forward the incomplete reformation begun by Elijah, he also shows his authority from on high. And so if the death of Christ and his ascension on high must occur before the wide spread of the gospel, his apostles, who had an extraordinary commission to the world, and who have furnished us with the most important written records of revelation, go forth with like powers to those exerted by him, whom all they consent to call Master. And only because the church stands upon a foundation of unshaken truth can we account for the remarkable fact, which would certainly not be found in a system supported by credulity and imposture, that in proportion as the church grew strong and well established and able to palm false miracles upon the world, even the claim to exercise such gifts was less frequently made. The claim has been made in darker, later times, when the nature of the miracles and the proof of their occurrence are both in contrast with the earlier history. It seems likely that the power of working miracles largely existed in the Christian church during the first century, at least during the entire life-time of Christ's last Apostle; between that time and the conversion of Constantine the Great, we cannot certainly decide that all were spurious; but after the conversion of the Roman emperor, the only event of a miraculous nature that seems truly authenticated, is one wrought by Providence rather than by man—the Emperor Julian was divinely prevented from rebuilding the temple at Jerusalem.* Different writers in the Christian church testify to the cessation of miraculous powers. Gregory of New Cesarea in the third century was surnamed Thaumaturgus, because of the many wonders assigned to him; but none of his writings have descended to us, and his life comes to us only in the credulous narrative of a writer in the next century after him.† But Chrysostom, in the latter part of the fourth century, expressly says that "God has now ceased to work miracles;" and that "The gifts of the Spirit had ceased long ago."‡ And Theodoret § in the

* See Mosheim, 4th Cent., Neander, ii. 50. Warburton's Div. Leg., iii. 420. On the other side Lardner, vii. 604, seq.

† See Lardner, ii. 639, 640. Mosheim, Cent. iii., Pt. ii., ch. ii.: § vii.

‡ Lardner, iv. 566, 567. § Lardner, v. 21. See also v. 121, 123.

early part of the same century confirms the Scriptural miracles; but speaks as if these powers had ceased in his time.

It is easy to see how different these things are from the claim that miraculous powers belong to the church of God through long ages; and that the exercise of them is one of the marks of a true church.* When God gives an extraordinary commission and new teachings, it is according to his usual dealings to give these proofs of the Divine sanction.

V. The effects produced by the Miracles recorded in the Scriptures are an important part of the evidence that they were really wrought.

So Origen long ago argued that the alleged wonders of heathenism had left no traces behind them in the world's history; while the miracles of Moses issued in the Jewish polity; and those of the Lord Jesus established the Christian church.† So Chrysostom says that the spread of Christianity without a miracle would be greatly more miraculous than any thing recorded in the New Testament.‡ Nor can any man account for the influence gained by Moses over the Jews, except by believing that he had this Divine commission. Not because he flattered them, or laid light burdens upon them; not because they relished his laws, or that his writings agreed with the national

* See Milner's End of Controversy, Letter xxiii.

† Trench, 30.

‡ Lardner, iv., 563.

temper; on the contrary, ever rebelling against their own laws, ever apostatizing from their own religion, ever indulging a national temper widely different from their sacred books, we can only account for their unswerving testimony in favour of Moses for over three thousand years, by recognizing that he gave them at the time, incontestable proof of his Divine commission. And the argument to prove the Divine authority of Moses and of the entire Old Testament should be esteemed complete when the authority of Jesus Christ is established: seeing that he so explicitly acknowledges the claims and correctness of the Scriptures as held by the Jews of his times.

The stupendous fabric of Christianity must be accounted for, in the world's history. What it is, we know; and that its doctrines are unpalatable to the mass of men. Where and when it sprang up, we know; and that the obscure and despised people, from whose midst it came, had no power to withstand the forces they opposed. And be it remembered that even the infidel Gibbon could not reckon the causes of the spread of this religion without reckoning among them the *virtues* of the early Christians;* forgetting the inference that if they were virtuous men, they made no false claims in the world. There is no room here to speak of a mistaken sincerity. The workers and the witnesses of miracles like these, all knew,

* Reason and Faith, 370; note.

to a certainty, whether these things did, or did not occur. And when we consider the character of that age; the number of persons concerned; the innumerable wonders performed; the sacrifices, sufferings, and deaths endured; the mingled ignorance and originality of the early preachers; the scenes of their labours, in the proudest cities of the world; the fierce and continual opposition they encountered; and their rapid and permanent success, we have a stupendous aggregate of arguments, piled up to strengthen the miraculous foundation of Christianity, which may allow us to answer the unbeliever in the words of Chrysostom, "What miracle dost thou desire, oh man, beyond this great change made in the world all on a sudden."* In like manner Augustine argues, "If you do not believe the miracles, you must believe this miracle, that the world was converted without a miracle."†

* Lardner, iv. 564.

† Trench, 50 n.

CHAPTER XV.

THE MAGICIANS OF EGYPT.

THE long wished for day of Israelitish deliverance seems now about to dawn; the prayers of an enslaved people seem about to be answered; and they thankfully rejoice at the coming of Moses and Aaron. But God, even in the hour of fulfilling his promises, works not as man anticipates. Though Moses and Aaron are leaders sent by Jehovah, they are hindered in bringing God's chosen covenant people from the land of bondage. Rather, the immediate effect of their interposition is the increasing of Israelitish burdens; and the people murmured that heavier tasks resulted from the effort for deliverance.

Nor is it a transient or insignificant lesson that is taught us by these facts. Never is any great and needed change effected in moral or social life without the temporary creation of evils apparently greater than those before endured, preparatory to lasting benefits. Especially the leading forth of Israel from Egypt is typical of that great change which delivers the soul of man from Satan's bondage, and brings him into the liberty of Christ.

How many, in the change from nature to grace, partake of an experience, like this of Israel in Egypt. So long as the soul is the willing, indifferent, careless servant of Satan, it is left by him in comparative ease. The man may know his sinful estate, and may sometimes feel galled by his chains. But his mind is usually but little troubled. If at this time the message of God calls him to deliverance—as Moses and Aaron stood before the people in bondage—if the truth comes home to his conscience, it is to make him feel his bondage more grievously than ever before. It is not only that thoughts of freedom make him restive under servitude; but the great adversary lays heavier burdens upon him. How few enter in at the strait gate, except—to refer to Bunyan's graphic descriptions—they fall into the Slough of Despond, or are put in great fear, by the fierce barking of Beelzebub's dogs, or by the sharp-shooting of his archers. Yet these things are no disproof of approaching deliverance. As the Israelites murmured at the very things which in the end proved the care of their covenant God, so souls are perplexed and discouraged under teachings and experiences, which, properly understood, are evidences of Divine care. From first to last in a religious life, God's people must "walk by faith;" i. e. they must learn to trust his word whose teachings are plain, rather than be influenced by those dark providences through which, as yet, we cannot see.

But though the troubled soul is often told these things by his teachers and by the sacred word, he is like one who hears not. Like the oppressed Israelites, when Pharaoh laid heavier burdens upon them, he hearkens not to the voice of instruction "for anguish of spirit and for cruel bondage." Ex. vi. 9. So Bunyan quaintly says that "twenty thousand cart-loads, yea millions of wholesome instructions"—"the best materials to make good the ground of the place,"—have been cast into the Slough of Despond; "yet it is the Slough of Despond still, and so will be when they have done what they can."

But we may now properly give our attention to the important scenes, which are transacted before the king of Egypt to induce him to let Israel go. When we reflect that Divine power could so easily have made the covenant people victorious in a fierce battle with their oppressors, and have sent them forth triumphant in the hour of victory, we should easily judge that purposes of great wisdom are involved in the dealings of God with Egypt. Jehovah here displays his power to baffle the deepest designs of man; and executes his purposes at the same time that the wickedness of man is allowed to plan and to work to its utmost efficiency. And doubtless among the chief of the Divine designs in this memorable contest, is his purpose to show the vanity and weakness of the gods of Egypt; to pour contempt upon them and upon their boasted power; and to prove himself the God of all the earth. So before the close of this series of terrible judgments upon the land for its idolatry, Jehovah expressly declares, "Against all the gods of Egypt will I execute judgment." Ex. xii. 12.

When Moses and Aaron stood before the king, they made at first the moderate demand that he would allow them to go three days' journey into the desert to sacrifice. We need not say that there was anything disingenuous in this demand, even when we allow that ultimately they aimed at their complete deliverance. For as obedience to the Divine will in small matters often prepares a man to yield obedience in greater things, so, had Pharaoh granted this permission for a slight indulgence, and afterwards cheerfully gone beyond his first grant, no one would charge Moses with deception, because his first demand had not opened up his whole mind. And it is plain, that Pharaoh's unwillingness to grant even this much, is clearer proof of his rebellion against Jehovah, than if from the first Moses had proposed the full emancipation of the people.

The second appearance of Moses and Aaron before the king was attended by the exhibition of those miraculous signs by which they were to prove their commission from the God of heaven. Delaying to consider these wonders themselves until a subsequent chapter, we now occupy our thoughts with the nature of the miracles here apparently ascribed to the Egyptian magicians. In almost all lands and ages, we read of an order of men making supernatural pretensions; from the magicians of Egypt to the Chaldean astrologers and the African sorcerers and rain-makers. And here we find Pharaoh calling for the magicians to work like wonders to those shown by Moses; as his predecessor had sent for the same class of men to interpret his dreams before he knew of Joseph, Gen. xli. 8; and as the king of Babylon did before he knew Daniel. Dan. ii. 2. The names of two of the Egyptian magicians, Jannes and Jambres, are recorded for us by the Apostle Paul. 2 Tim. iii. 8.

But the chief matter of interest in regard to these wonders wrought before Pharaoh, relates to the power of these magicians. Various opinions exist among commentators respecting the questions, Did these men really work miracles? Or was their part of the contest carried on merely by deception, jugglery, and sleight of hand?

Several remarks may engage our attention before we consider the reasons urged for the opposite opinions.

1st. It may seem a strange thing that the inspired narrative does not settle this question beyond the possibility of doubt as to the meaning. Why are not the magicians branded as impostors, if so they were? In reply we may notice this peculiarity of the entire Bible, that events are simply recorded, without any expression of opinion upon them; leaving the readers to understand the events, from principles elsewhere expressed, or from their connections or results. The Apostles scarcely express their indignation at the wickedness of Judas, in betraying, or of the Jews, in crucifying Jesus: they scarcely express surprise at the wonders of Divine power and grace around them. In the simplest and most impartial manner, the Scriptures record words and events as they appeared before those who saw and heard them. And thus Moses records the apparent doings of the magicians; knowing that the result of the whole contest was a sufficient proof of their "manifest" weakness and "folly." 2 Tim. iii. 9.

2d. It is well known that in all ages of the world, and even in our own times, many strange things have been wrought which it is impossible for us fully to explain. The magic of the ancients is sometimes divided into three classes, natural, artificial, and diabolical. Natural magic consists in performing such wonders as an ignorant audience may ascribe to supernatural power, but which truly result from a superior knowledge of natural philosophy. Artificial magic is the working of wonders by jugglery or sleight of hand. Diabolical magic was such as was wrought by the aid of evil spirits.

We are very certain that evil spirits were permitted, in former ages, to possess the bodies of men; and it may be to work wonders, such as man could not effect without an agency beyond his own.

The teachings of the New Testament are explicit upon this point; and from its narratives, it would appear that Satan possessed unwonted power among men at the very time when our Lord Jesus Christ was upon the earth. As he came to destroy the works of the devil, so never were there so many demoniacal possessions as then. And it is very remarkable indeed, that, as if the oracles of the heathen were pronounced by the aid of Satanic influence, we hear in those times the voice of Paganism lamenting that they had no longer the power of their utterance. So Juvenal,* a famous Roman satirist of this period, complains that the heathen oracles had ceased. The anger of the gods because of the spread of Christianity was a frequent method of accounting for existing evils; and even the infidel Porphyry, when no stop could be put to a contagious and desolating sickness, assigned as a cause for it, that by reason of the spread of Christianity, the influence of Esculapius upon the earth was over.† Several heathen writers say that the oracle at Delphi ceased through the influence of a Hebrew boy.‡ How much in the utterances of these oracles was by the deceit and imposture of the priests, and how much by any

* "Quoniam Delphis oracula cessant,
Et genus humanum, damnat caligo futuri."
Satires vi. 555–6.

† Neander's Church History, i. 92.

‡ Edwards' Hist. Red. Works, i. 448.

other agency, we cannot determine. And we may say the same of all that ever has been, or is now, called by the name of magic. Some things are unquestionably deception; and some things we are not able to explain from any knowledge that mankind as yet possesses of the powers of nature. Yet there is a wide difference between the acknowledgment that we cannot explain a phenomenon, and the recognition that it is supernatural, or, as some say, infranatural.

A 3d remark is that some of the tricks that are even now accomplished by the Egyptian jugglers greatly resemble the first and chief wonder wrought by the magicians before Pharaoh. When we notice that but three things were done by them; and that to produce skilfully a quantity of blood when so much was before them, and a few frogs when the land was full of them, does not surpass a juggler's cunning; the chief wonder wrought by them is the turning of their rods into serpents. It is certainly a singular coincidence that just this thing is now done by the Psylli, or serpent charmers of Egypt. These men constitute a distinct and hereditary "*guild*" among the Egyptians. They discover and remove serpents from the houses they infest; they play with them, and wrap them around their persons; and the French scholars, who accompanied Napoleon into Egypt, report that they profess to turn a snake into a stick. The serpent they use in this trick they call haje.

When they want to produce this effect, they spit into its throat, close its mouth, and lay the reptile down. The snake then becomes stiff and motionless, and lies as if dead, and they are able to wake it up when they wish.*

* Kurtz's Old Cov. ii. 261. Hengstenberg's Books of Moses, 141. Serpent-charming in Smith's Dict.

CHAPTER XVI.

THE NATURE OF THEIR MAGICAL WONDERS.

"The world had much of strange and wonderful:
In passion much, in action, reason, will,
And much in providence which still retired
From human eye." POLLOK.

THE opinion that the magicians before Pharaoh wrought no real miracles, but only practised deceptive arts, is not a new one, springing up either from the superior light, or the advancing skepticism, of later days. It is an ancient view of the case. Josephus speaks of their wonders as done by craft and by counterfeiting true things. In the Book of Wisdom, confessedly ancient, their works are called "the illusions of art magic." xvii. 17.

One chief reason for supposing that these men wrought no miracles, is drawn from the apparent inconsistency that God would allow them thus to withstand his own servants, and to succeed in practising things whose tendency was to harden the hearts of their people against the truth. Yet obviously we are unable to determine how far the arts of deception may be carried. We cannot deny that men deceive each other, and in the most important affairs. The servants of God in all ages have found their chief trials in the oppositions of false teachers, who make fair professions of truthfulness and sincerity: the great adversary of souls, if not by his immediate agency, yet by various means, gains access to the hearts of men, and succeeds in his efforts to deceive them. Especially those who love evil, are often given up to believe a lie. It is therefore quite impossible for us to say how far this deception may be carried; and since God allows sin to exist and Satan to work, we cannot say that this or that manifestation of evil is inconsistent with the Divine goodness.

Another reason for judging that the magicians practised only deception and jugglery is the difficulty of allowing that any power, except that of God, can work these wonders. And truly this is a formidable objection, if either we are to understand that the work of creation was wrought by them ; or that they attained to the higher order of miracles Yet transformation is not equivalent to creation. We shall soon see that their wonders were far inferior to those of Moses and Aaron, even if it be granted that the power they exerted was more than belongs to the unaided abilities of man.

On the whole it seems more in accordance with the terms of the inspired narrative to suppose, that these men did work wonders in the presence of Pharaoh, surpassing the mere power of man. The plain letter of the narrative sustains this idea: the influence upon Pharaoh was just what the actual working of such prodigies would produce; so to understand it only involves the same difficulties which we otherwise find in the providence of God: and the Scriptures recognize the existence of false miracles and false prophets. So there are other things in the world as inexplicable to us as the wonders thus ascribed to them.

Yet in either view of the case, even when the most astonishing power is ascribed to them that can be justified by the terms of the narrative, these things may be said to vindicate the providence of God in allowing the false prophets of Egypt to oppose those whom God had sent upon an important mission, the true prophets of Israel.

1st. The Scriptures always speak of these and like things in subsequent history as *lying* wonders. So Paul says of these men that their folly was made manifest. 2 Tim. iii. 9. So Moses speaks of those who work signs and wonders in favour of false gods; and declares that this is of itself sufficient proof of evil. Deut. xiii. 2–5. Our Lord Jesus Christ declares, that false Christs and false prophets should show great signs and wonders, sufficiently delusive to deceive the very elect, (Matt. xxiv. 24,) if that was a possible thing! And Paul says of the Great Apostasy that through the working of Satan it would possess power to work signs and lying wonders. 2 Thess. ii. 9. In all these things there seems implied the power at least to deceive men; and to secure this deception by mingled power and imposture. The limits of the two, we cannot accurately define. But it is worthy of distinct notice that the Scriptures ascribe these things always to evil; say they are credited by men through the liability of unrighteous hearts to be deceived; and call them expressly LYING WONDERS. Even if the wonders are not themselves wholly false, they tend to support falsehood. In their end, if not in their nature, oftentimes in both, this is their solution; they are lying wonders.

2d. The opposition of these magicians to Moses and Aaron had the effect of causing these men themselves to become witnesses for the Divine authority of the legitimate prophets. When in the days of his flesh, our Lord Jesus cleansed the lepers of Israel, he always sent them to the priests to be pronounced clean. By this, two things were accomplished. (1) The leper was formally admitted to his standing in society by the proper authority; and (2) The very priests, who were the best judges of leprosy and its cure, and at the same time the most resolute adversaries of Christ, were made the witnesses that a miracle had really been wrought. Who could question that he had cleansed the leper, when his very enemies had pronounced him clean? So in the days of Moses, the very miracle-workers of Egypt bear testimony to the prophet's power. Had they not been called into Pharaoh's presence at all, the king and his people might have regarded Moses and Aaron as only wonder-workers, whose skill somewhat surpassed the men they were wont to see. Had the magicians come with no power to do anything, even as they were accustomed to do, the God of Moses might have been esteemed by the idolatrous Egyptians as no more true than their own gods, but only as possessing superior power. But these men, whose entire profession was devoted to maintain the idolatry of Egypt were divinely allowed to come before the king, and there perform the utmost arts which they ever professed to practise elsewhere. Thus they were fully committed to a contest between themselves and God's prophets; and no room was left to evade the subsequent comparison between them. If ever these men wrought wonders, it was in the wisdom of Providence that upon this occasion they should be allowed to do their utmost.

3d. It is carefully to be noticed, that these magicians do nothing, that they attempt nothing AGAINST the working of Moses and Aaron. The contest is unequal from the beginning. The lying wonders are never equal, in nature or in evidence, to the true miracles, as we read the usual records of history. It had been an object well worthy of the true strength of these magicians, to counteract the miracles of Moses. When he turned the Nile to blood, why did they not pity the horror and distress of their suffering people, and turn it back to water? When Moses brought frogs upon the land, why did they not banish the plague from the borders of Egypt? Such works as these would have been worthy of their real power. But they were able, in the largest exertion of their power, only to multiply the miseries of the land; and instead of taking sides with Pharaoh, they coöperate with Moses and Aaron in increasing the plagues of the guilty king.

And 4th. Throughout the entire contest, the superiority of Moses and Aaron plainly appears. Aaron's rod swallowed up their rods. And all they attempt is inferior, and soon at an end. It seems not difficult for skilful sleight of hand to produce blood in a vessel, when the river is already full of it; or to produce frogs, when the land is oppressed by their multitude: but it is not long till their skill is baffled by wonders that seem no more difficult to accomplish; they are constrained to acknowledge that this power surpasses theirs; and as they retire confounded from the contest, and even unable to free their own persons from the plagues upon the land, their lips are sealed from all cavillings against the mission of these prophets.

5th. It is important for us to notice the teachings, here and elsewhere, of these sacred Scriptures, that the influence of these wonders wrought to support evil is chiefly owing to the state of heart in the beholders. Honest, truth-loving men are not liable to be deceived by these things. And this honesty of mind and purpose, is not exactly the same thing as sincerity of belief. Deception and hypocrisy are not the same thing; though it is true that something of both is usually found in the supporters of error. When men profess a system of lies and use their earnest efforts to maintain and promote it, it may be true, that they really believe it. The apostate church of Rome, no doubt, embraces many sincere believers, who are none the less wrong for all their sincerity. The language of Paul is very strong respecting the errors, which he predicts in the latter times. He says, God shall send them "strong delusions that they should believe a lie." 2 Thess. ii. 11. He speaks of those who are deceivers at the same time that they are themselves deceived. But some measure of sincere belief is implied in the very idea of deceit. It is only when we believe a false thing to be true, that we are deceived by it. We cannot be deceived by that which we do not at all regard as true. In a deceived heart there may be many misgivings, yet a thing known to be false ceases, so far, to be deceptive.

But in judging of the moral condition of those who are thus deceived, we must especially notice to what their deception is chiefly due. And the Scriptures abundantly teach that men are allowed to believe lies, because of their own wicked hatred of truth and love of falsehood. According to their teachings, it is an easy thing for falsehood to deceive a wicked heart. When men love their sins, they are easily persuaded to believe those doctrines that favour them. An expressive phrase indeed is that of Paul, the "deceivableness of unrighteousness." Unrighteous men are easily deceived. No men believe upon less evidence, or even plausibility of right, than those who receive the grossest errors. So Paul declares those men who are given up of God to believe lies, received not the love of the truth; believed not the truth; and had pleasure in unrighteousness.

The wonders wrought before Pharaoh would all have been rejected, in comparison with the superior wonders wrought by Moses and Aaron, but for the pride and rebellion of his heart against truth and against God. And this is true of all the lying wonders of the world's history. Wrought to support systems of falsehood; destitute usually of any just evidences of their superior origin, they are credited only by those who receive them by tradition without investigation, and by those who are willing to be deceived. It sufficiently accounts for the belief of false miracles, and for the easy spread of false doctrines, and for the opposition constantly made to the truth, that the minds of sinful men are averse to truth; they do not like to retain God in their knowledge; they love darkness rather than light. And the triumphs of the gospel of Christ in every place show abundantly, that the reason why men oppose the spread of its principles is chiefly the rebellion of wicked hearts against holy truths. No man can give an intelligent reason for the bitter and constant opposition of infidels to the church of God, unless he takes into the account that instinctive antipathy which wrong has against right. Error of every form in Christian lands is more in the heart than in the intellect; hundreds of men are ready to give up at once their doctrinal errors, as soon as they are ready to give up their sins; and the humble cry of a sinner to a Divine Saviour, is better than the most learned arguments, against heresy. So the Apostle appropriately warns us, "Take heed, brethren, lest there be in any of you an *evil heart* of unbelief in departing from the living God." Heb. iii. 12. How easy a thing for any man to arrive at knowledge of the highest importance concerning God and salvation, if he would but begin the earnest careful practice of those simple duties he already knows. So the Saviour says, "If any man will do his will he shall know of the doctrine." John vii. 17. "If any one cannot fully see, let him not wait, but go forward, earnestly seeking to serve God, and the truth shall be made plain to him."* "Then shall we know if we follow on to know the Lord." Hosea vi. 3. How different is this humble teachable temper, from the spirit of pride in Pharaoh, we shall afterwards see.

* Jacobus on John, 132.

CHAPTER XVII.

THE EARLIER PLAGUES UPON EGYPT.

"The lawless tyrant, who denies
To know their God, or message to regard,
Must be compelled by signs and judgments dire."
MILTON.

THE first miracle wrought before Pharaoh to establish the Divine commission of the Israelitish prophets failed to influence the mind of the king. He refused to let the people go. The subsequent miracles therefore became a series of judgments to scourge him and his guilty land; and to compel the release of the sons of Jacob. No more remarkable instance of hardened rebellion against God is recorded in human history: and after knowing what God did to Pharaoh and Egypt, no sinful man, or sinful people, need ever expect success in warring against their Maker.

It is well worthy of our notice that the miraculous plagues wrought by Moses in the land of Egypt, have what may be called a natural aspect in that land. Some of these things are peculiar to that country, and frequently occur there as natural phenomena, well known to the people. Moses turned the waters of the river to blood; and brought frogs and flies and locusts and darkness upon the land. But the Nile, nearly every year turns red like blood at the time of its overflowings, because the red marl of the higher districts discolours the water through the force of the stream: frogs and flies and locusts are objects familiar to the Egyptians; and the Sirocco, which blows over Egypt from the great desert of Sahara, often covers the whole country with a horrible darkness that compels the inhabitants to shut themselves up in their houses. Now because these are natural phenomena in Egypt, greatly resembling the wonders ascribed in the sacred narrative to Moses and Aaron, skeptical writers have objected to the whole narrative as plainly an exaggerated account of the occurrences that really took place at the time of the Exodus. As modern historians rank among mythological fables a large portion of early profane history, so are many disposed to rank these earlier historical records of the Hebrews, among the mythical narratives which have but the shadow of a foundation in historical truth.

Reserving to a subsequent chapter the statement of the remarkable proof which sustains historically the entire claims of the books of Moses, we may now take occasion to offer a few remarks touching the miracles of Egypt.

1st. No difference can be more important than

that which we may mark between the book of Exodus and those portions of ancient history assigned by capable historians to the mythological periods. In no single instance do the writers of those histories claim that they record what they themselves saw; or even the occurrences of their own age or land. It is an easy thing to indulge in exaggeration, when writing of ages long past, known to us only by dim traditions, and magnified in their importance by a spirit of national pride. But no instance can be pointed out, of a man's writing the history of his own times, which was received by his own people, and handed down to succeeding times as true, when really he had not given, in the main, a fair statement of the case. That Moses wrote this history during the life-time of thousands who saw the events he has recorded; and especially that his history is in no wise flattering to the Jewish people in whose care he left it, should suffice to free these historical records from any charge of exaggeration.

2d. The very fact that these miracles wrought in Egypt possess a natural, rather than an unnatural, aspect is a valid argument to support the claim that they were the results of Divine power and wisdom. We have before noticed the tendency of false wonders to be rather prodigies and monsters than miracles. The miracles of the Scriptures are *supernatural* but not *un*natural. That God should use the phenomena with which the

Egyptians were already acquainted to scourge their rebellion and wickedness, is better evidence of his interposition, than if the narrative related things entirely beyond the sphere of their acquaintance.

3d. There are sufficient proofs that these events, though analogous to natural events, were still miraculous. This proof arises from the time of their coming and going, so evidently at the bidding of Moses: from their so wonderfully exceeding the effects which natural causes alone could produce: from the attendant circumstances, which can be ascribed only to the Divine interposition: and from the singular fact, that the Israelites, though dwelling in the same land, were exempted from the curse of the severest plagues. When not only these events occur as Moses bade, but when he even allows the king himself to choose the time of their removal;* when the Nile becomes loathsome, and unheard of swarms of reptiles and insects come in such rapid succession; when the arts of the magicians fail, and they also must recognize the finger of God, and even are unable to free themselves from suffering with the other Egyptians, Ex. ix. 11; when the Israelites are so separated from the Egyptians; and when the Egyptians themselves no longer feel such plagues as soon as the contest is ended between Pharaoh and Moses; the entire truthfulness of the narrative can alone

* Shuckford, ii. 232.

be made to consist with the design of the record. To destroy the miraculous nature of these transactions is to stultify the whole narrative.

4th. To all which we may briefly add, that the principal objectors of modern times to the credibility of the Scriptural miracles have succeeded only in proposing theories more perplexing than the simple belief of Divine interposition for ends so important. If it be possible to explain *some* of the miracles as strange events, not supernatural, yet to attempt this explanation of all would be to exhibit an aggregate of natural things, exceedingly strange in themselves; yet not thought either natural or strange in this sense, by those who witnessed them; and still no good reason assigned for their occurrence or record in this connection; the whole history, if Divine interposition be stricken out, being aimless and incongruous; to use the trite illustration, the play of Hamlet, Hamlet himself omitted. Or if again we look at the theory of myths, how can we explain the reception of Jesus of Nazareth as the Jewish Messiah? His cotemporary disciples must have known whether he did or did not work miracles, and otherwise fulfil the Old Testament predictions of the Christ. Wonders increase rather than diminish, if we must believe that they first gave up all their Jewish ideas to become this man's disciples, and then gradually formed their conceptions of him and expressed in the gospels what the great Teacher should have done.

We speak indiscriminately of Old and New Testament miracles; for if either be true, both are.

The first miracle of judgment upon the Egyptians was the turning of the Nile to a river of blood. This sight of horror should at once have gained the consent of the proud king that Israel should go forth from the land. The esteem in which the Egyptians have ever held the Nile, it is hard for us to realize. That noble river, flowing to them from the distant interior of their continent, not only beautified the land, but was the chief source of its unparalleled fertility. Rain seldom falls in Egypt; the overflowings of the river is their only dependence for watering the soil; and they determine the prospects of their crops from the height of the inundation. The water of the Nile also has long been celebrated for its excellence, for drinking. Not only is it almost the only water in Egypt fit to drink; but the inhabitants of the country are extravagant in their praises of it: when absent from home, they talk much of the pleasure of drinking the Nile water upon their return; the Turks enjoy it so much that they eat salt to provoke a greater thirst; and it is a common saying among them, that if Mohammed had tasted the Nile water, he would have prayed for an earthly immortality that he might drink it for ever.*

The Nile also was a god to the Egyptians.

* Kurtz's Hist. Old Covenant, ii. 273.

Their monuments call it the god Nile, the life-giving father of all that exists. Upon this venerated river came the first of the judgments by which Moses scourged the land. And this judgment was two-fold.

1st. It avenged the cruelty of the Egyptians towards Israel. Into this sacred stream the Egyptians had ruthlessly cast the babes of Israel; eighty years ago this same Moses had himself been subject to this sanguinary edict, and owed his strange preservation to the care of Israel's covenant God: and as they themselves had defiled its stream with innocent blood, the prophet stretches his rod over it to repay their cruelty by this fearful plague.

2d. Thus their idolatry was rebuked. Even their gods met with the judgments of him, who proves himself the Lord in the land. The pride of Egypt rolls before them a pestilential flood; they must dig in the earth for water to quench their thirst; even their magicians have power only to make the matter worse, and are unable to remove the curse from the Nile, or to make a portion of its waters fit to drink. If we suppose, with some interpreters, that the seven days named, refer to the length of time that elapsed between the first and the second judgments, then we cannot decide how long this wonder lasted. Yet it was long enough to show the reality of the miracle; and the dying of the fish in the river, and the loathsomeness of the water, seemed sufficiently to distinguish this, from the mere discolouring of the annual flood.

As frogs abound in the marshy borders of the Nile, an extraordinary increase of these reptiles formed the second plague. As a frog-headed god and goddess are found among the Egyptian divinities, we may justly regard this also as a punishment for their idolatry; and they are troubled by their own gods. The innumerable hordes of frogs, coming up upon everything, filling up every place, defiling their very beds and their food, must have been greatly distressing and disgusting. The ovens of the Egyptians were merely small holes in the ground, filled with their scanty fuel, where they baked for a single meal in an earthen vessel; and these would of course be filled with these active reptiles. We need not be surprised that the magicians imitated this infliction; the slightest skill in jugglery could produce frogs when the land was so full of them. It is a more surprising thing, that when Moses allowed Pharaoh to fix his own time for the removal of this curse, he should be willing to wait until the next day. We would think in such a case, the sooner the better. But perhaps the stern king hoped that even this curse was from some natural cause; and that perhaps the frogs would depart at some different time and of themselves, to the discomfiture of the Jewish prophets.

Many learned interpreters understand that the next plague was not *lice*, but gnats, or mosquitoes. These insects greatly abound in Egypt, and are mentioned by Herodotus, who also mentions the mosquito bars of the ancient inhabitants.* It is said that, without exception, the irritation of the sting of the mosquito-gnat is the most intolerable of insect plagues.† This miracle the magicians could not even imitate. They acknowledged the finger of God, retired from the unequal contest, and appear no more in these scenes, except as afterwards they also become sufferers, and are unable to relieve even their own persons from the judgments which Moses pronounces.

The fourth plague is remarkable for the exemption given from this time forward to the children of Israel. In this is distinctly marked the design of all these judgments, to vindicate the name of the Lord, and to deliver his people from bondage. There was nothing in the nature of these judgments to give exemption to the land of Goshen. The lightning might strike there as well as upon the Egyptians; the winged plagues might easily cross the Nile to them; and there was great significance in their lighted dwellings while all Egypt groped through that preternatural darkness. It is no wonder that the heart of Pharaoh at times relented, and that he seemed half dis-

* ii. § 95. Yet our *nets* are finer to secure the end.

† Bush.

posed to yield the contest. Yet with amazing fortitude in a cause so bad and hopeless, he still refused to let Israel go, until the popular will could no longer be repressed, even by the power of an absolute sovereign; and Moses and his people went forth from the land in triumph.

CHAPTER XVIII.

LOCUSTS AND DARKNESS.

"Onward they come, a dark continuous cloud
Of congregated myriads numberless;
The rushing of whose wings was as the sound
Of some broad river, headlong in its course,
Plunged from a mountain summit; or the roar
Of the wild ocean in the autumnal storm
Shattering its billows on a shore of rocks."

SOUTHEY.

In our version of the Scriptures the fourth plague upon Egypt is said to be swarms of flies. Yet with their characteristic fidelity the translators mark the ambiguity of the original by italicising the words "*of flies;*" thus denoting the absence of the words in the original. In Ps. lxxviii. 45, the same word is rendered "divers sorts of flies."* Interpreters are divided in sentiment respecting the creatures really meant. The Jewish writers generally suppose that a mixed multitude of creatures is meant. Others suppose that they were creeping insects, as they are said to be upon the ground. Ex. viii. 21. Especially they regard this plague as a visitation of the scarabæus or sacred beetle, which was

* So the Douay here.

among the sacred emblems of the Egyptians. Figures of this sacred insect are found, cut upon their ancient tombs, and sometimes with hieroglyphic descriptions. Even their embalmed bodies have been discovered at Thebes. A remarkable colossal figure of this beetle, cut out of a block of green granite, is now placed in the British Museum. But in regard to this fourth plague Dr. J. A. Alexander says, "The best interpreters are now agreed that it means the Egyptian dog-fly, which Philo represents as feeding upon flesh and blood."* The plague was so severely felt that Pharaoh made some concession to the demands of Moses, even agreeing to let the people go, "not very far away;" and thus secured the removal of the evil.†

Plagues were now sent upon the cattle of the Egyptians; then upon their persons; then upon their growing crops. In suffering these, the king vacillated; now almost led to endure these things no longer; now proudly resolving still to resist. When Moses therefore openly declared that a

* On Ps. lxxviii. 45.

† In the London Athenæum lately, there was a notice of some beautiful Egyptian jewelry, open at the London International Exhibition, taken from a tomb at Gournah by M. Mariette in 1859. Among other articles was "a collar of gold, having depending from it three flies of solid gold. There is little doubt that this is the decoration of the ancient Egyptian honorary Order of the Fly, whose origin is unknown." Perhaps the "Order" is an offspring of an antiquary's fruitful imagination: but the relic proves that the fly was reverenced, as the other ornaments described are symbols of their idolatry.

flight of locusts should come up, more disastrous than had ever been known in their past history, the servants of Pharaoh, aware by experience that the words of Moses would be fulfilled, and fearing for the utter destruction of Egypt, joined to entreat the king that he would let the people go. The haughty monarch sought another compromise, by allowing the men to go, and retaining the women as hostages for their return. But Moses firmly declared that they should go forth with everything, women, children, and cattle. And he was driven forth from the presence of Pharaoh.

All authorities join to declare the wonderful destruction and desolation that follow the devastations of a cloud of locusts. The astonishing numbers in which these insects fly, the noise they make as they devour every green thing, and the miserable condition to which they reduce a flourishing country, every writer declares. They are doubtless the most formidable insects in the world. The prophet Joel describes them in language exceedingly graphic and terrific, "A fire devoureth before them, and behind them a flame burneth: the land is as the garden of Eden before them, and behind them a desolate wilderness; yea and nothing shall escape them. The appearance of them is as the appearance of horses, and as horsemen so shall they run. Like the noise of chariots on the tops of mountains shall they leap, like the noise of a flame of fire that devoureth the stubble, as a strong people set in battle array. Before their face the people shall be much pained: all faces shall gather blackness. They shall run like mighty men, they shall climb the wall like men of war; and they shall march every one on his ways. . . . They shall run to and fro in the city; . . . they shall climb up upon the houses; they shall enter in at the windows like a thief." Joel ii. 3—9.

How remarkably like this Scriptural description are the words of the French infidel, Volney. "One would imagine," he writes, "that fire had followed their progress. Wherever their myriads spread, the verdure of the country disappears; trees and plants stripped of their leaves, and reduced to their naked boughs and stems, cause the dreary image of winter to succeed in an instant to the rich scenery of spring."* And he speaks of the heavens being literally obscured with their flight. Other writers and travellers give similar statements. Barrow states that in Southern Africa the ground was covered with them to an area of 2000 square miles; and that the water of a very wide river was scarcely visible for the floating carcasses.† Such inconceivable numbers often breed pestilence by the stench arising from their dead bodies. Augustine says that 800,000 people in Numidia were carried off by a pestilence having such an origin;‡ and many more in the neighbour-

* Bush, Ex. x. 13. † Encyclopedia Americana.

‡ Decivitate Dei, lib. iii. ch. xxxi.

ing coasts; and even in modern history in the Venitian territories in 1487, 30,000 perished by a plague that followed a visitation of locusts.* In 1748 these locusts came into Europe as far north as Germany, France and even England; but they perished in a short time and without doing any very serious injury.

So serious is the plague of locusts esteemed in the Sacred volume, that the Saracenic conquests are, in the book of Revelation, compared to the coming of a cloud of locusts to desolate the earth. Rev. ix.

We are not surprised then that the king hastened to call Moses and Aaron, when such a visitation as this came upon the land. And the deliverance was great. He had too good reason to fear that a pestilence would follow the destruction which he now witnessed; and that the worst of the plague therefore was still to come. But mercy was shown, even to him who had been so rebellious. A strong wind took up these clouds of locusts, and bore them away from Egypt, and cast them into the Red Sea. But though Egypt was thus spared from the entire judgment of the plague of locusts, the king was no sooner delivered from his apprehensions, than he forgot his confessions of sin and his promises of amendment; and dared still to rebel against the God of Israel.

The next plague was significant of the difference

* Scottish Chn. Herald, i. 28. See Land and Book, ii. 102, seq.

between Egypt and Israel rather than in itself so hard to bear. A gross and dense darkness covered all the land of Egypt, so that no man could stir abroad, and perhaps so dense and damp vapours accompanied it, that the ordinary fire and lights could not be kindled in their houses. So the apocryphal book of Wisdom says they were frightened with visions, and monsters and indeed every natural sound tortured them with fear; and no power of fire could give them light. But even if these things were not so, it was in most significant contrast, that all the land of Goshen was still in the light.

If we esteem this dreadful darkness as a natural phenomenon, miraculous only in its time and purpose and severity, we may regard it as the blowing of the Khamsin, or Egyptian Sirocco; the horrors of which are described by many travellers. This however is a dry wind. Some declare that during its prevalence the people are obliged to shut themselves up in their houses and even in cellars; and Rosenmueller in his commentary cites accounts from the middle ages according to which the Khamsin covered Egypt with such dense darkness "that every one thought the last day was at hand."* The Rev. Dr. Edward Robinson of New York experienced the effects of one of these Khamsins, in passing through Arabia, but it was of short duration, and he speaks of it as *resembling*

* Kurtz's Old Cov., ii. 287.

the Khamsin. The wind "blew a perfect tempest. The atmosphere was filled with fine particles of sand, forming a bluish haze; the sun was scarcely visible, his disk exhibiting only a dim and sickly hue; and the glow of the wind came upon our faces as from a burning oven. Often we could not see ten rods around us; and our eyes, ears, mouths and clothes were filled with sand."* He says he can well conceive that such a "horrible tempest" might prove fatal to a traveller previously feeble and exhausted. But if this wind accompanied the darkness of Egypt, still the miraculous nature of such a gloom was sufficiently plain. And here, as before, dishonour is thrown upon the Egyptian gods. They called their kings Pharaoh, deriving this from Phrah, the sun. For the sun was esteemed by them "not only one of the grandest works but one of the direct agents of the Deity;"† they attributed to him even a "participation of the Divine essence;" and the king bore his name, because he was the emblem of the god of light, and derived his royal authority directly from the gods. But now a god, so much worshipped by them, with offerings of incense three times a day, withholds his light from them; yet shines with undiminished splendour upon the dwellings of Goshen.

* Biblical Researches, ii. 288.

† Wilkinson's Ancient Egyptians, i. 328.

While then there does not seem to be so much of severity in this plague of darkness as in some of those that preceded it, we find the king ready again to offer a compromise to the Jewish prophets. He even sent for Moses and Aaron, and gave his consent that they and also their families might go; yet unwilling to make a surrender at discretion, he refuses to allow that they shall take their herds of cattle. But now Moses makes terms not hitherto proposed. Rising with the consciousness of both power and right, he demands that all shall be allowed to go; and that Pharaoh even shall give them burnt-offerings and sacrifices. To this Pharaoh will not agree. His anger rose above any previous occasion; and he drove the prophets from him, forbidding them ever again to enter his presence on the penalty of death.

During all this time the demeanour of Moses had been calm, dignified, and forbearing. His appearance doubtless was exceedingly venerable. Though a vigorous man, for forty years after this time, yet he was even now over eighty years of age: and, we may easily imagine, of a patriarchal presence. With all the power he exhibited in Egypt, there is no indication of pride; no assumption of honours not due to him. But now the haughty king has rejected the last solemn warning that was tempered with mercy. After any of the preceding plagues, his relentings would have spared Egypt. Now mercy ceases with his rude repulse of the Lord's messengers; and Moses declares that in obedience to his word, he will see his face no more. But before he departs from the king's presence, he addresses him with that tone of lofty and righteous indignation which the prophets of God have sometimes used towards the incorrigible in wickedness. He declares that that very night the first-born, in all the nation, and even in the palace, shall die; that lamentation shall rise throughout all the land, such as Egypt never before had known; that the Israelites shall be wholly exempt from this last and most fearful stroke; and that now, forbidden to see the face of the king, they should neither condescend nor need to ask permission to leave the land. The closing scene of the great contest in the wild uproar of the Red Sea's waves he does not as yet mention; but he declares that the Egyptians shall come and bow down before him, and urge him and the entire people speedily to get forth from the land.

CHAPTER XIX.

PHARAOH'S HARDENED HEART.

"How long may we go on in sin?
How long will God forbear?
Where does hope end; and where begin
The confines of despair?"

THE mysteries of the universe are innumerable. And in the expêrience of every thoughtful man these increase in numbers and in perplexity as he grows in knowledge. There is a sense indeed in which knowledge is the solving of mysteries; but the solution of one difficulty is effected by creating or revealing more and greater perplexities. The strange things which puzzled us in childhood, we now understand: but stranger things puzzle us now than then. We never thought at all in our youthful days of the things which now seem mysterious; and those things which through our increasing knowledge have ceased to perplex us, have with their loss of mystery lost also the power to interest our minds. After all, mystery is but another name for ignorance; and so long as some things remain unknown to us, mysteries cannot cease. There is but One Mind in the universe to which nothing is mysterious; for but One is infinite in wisdom and knowledge. Finite minds however high their capacities, or however large their knowledge, cannot fully know God, his ways or his works; and so must ever find knowledge to acquire, and mysteries to solve. In this lower world, we see more dimly than we shall hereafter. And yet even our perplexities are not without their use. If we are wise enough not to spend our strength upon impracticable things, the very difficulties that attend the pursuit of wisdom may awaken our energies to overcome them. It may indeed be carrying the matter quite too far to say, with some of the wise men of the world, that our searchings for truth are better than the actual possession of truth;* but doubtless many of the mysteries of the world around us are designed to lead us to an humble faith in that ever-blessed God, whom our highest searchings cannot find out; and many are intended to animate our activity in pressing eagerly after that knowledge which seems only larger and more desirable when we have gained the most of it.

Scarcely any more remarkable or instructive example of the dreadful strength and influence which sin may gain over the heart of man, can be found in all the history of the race, than we have here brought before us. See the king of Egypt resisting the plagues sent upon his land, and refus-

* See Sir Wm. Hamilton's Lectures, Lect. I., p. 7—9.

ing to let Israel go. As the Scriptures expressly declare that God raised up Pharaoh to show his power, and to declare his name through all the earth; and as the Apostle Paul brings his case plainly before us, as an example of the Divine Sovereignty, Ex. ix. 16, Rom. ix. 17, so it is our wisdom to learn from this case, how dreadful is our God, and how fearful and how foolish it is for man to stand in rebellion against him.

The Bible is remarkable for this, that its doctrinal statements are made in the plainest language, and that its illustrations are as strong as any that can possibly arise in the history of man. No man can teach the doctrine of God's sovereignty more plainly than we have it taught here; and no illustrations can be more in point to show the sinfulness of man in doing the predetermined counsel of God than are afforded by Pharaoh, and Judas, and the crucifiers of the Messiah. If we can reconcile the plain and Scriptural examples with the sovereignty of the Divine government, and with the entire freedom even of sinful man, we need not be perplexed with any of the practical difficulties that occur in any passing events of Providence.

There are two aspects in which the government of God over men is presented in the sacred Scriptures. In the first of these aspects it is unlimited and absolute. He doeth according to his will and pleasure; he taketh counsel of none; he hath mercy on whom he will have mercy; he hardeneth whom he will; and from the very perfection of that nature to which all things lie naked and open, his purposes are like himself, eternal and unchangeable. If any ruler can be of absolute and unlimited authority, such a government pertains to God. But in the *second aspect* of the Divine government it is a limited sovereignty; and this in such a sense as to add infinitely to its glory and excellency. The sovereignty of God is bounded, not by anything in his creatures; but by the perfections of his own character. The Scriptures reckon it among his excellencies that there are things he cannot do. He does his will; but that will is not capricious or arbitrary; it is ever wise, true, holy and just. So he cannot lie; cannot himself be tempted to evil; cannot tempt any man to sin; cannot deny the infinite perfections of his own character. It is not weakness, but strength and perfection in our glorious God, that lead him ever to govern himself by principles of truth and righteousness. He is absolute and free; because he is under the control of none; because he does his own pleasure; and yet we have the highest possible assurance that infinite wisdom and righteousness and truth belong to all he is, and to all he does.

The Scriptural doctrine of the Divine sovereignty is expressly placed in full harmony with the Divine righteousness. And so when the Apostle Paul teaches us this doctrine in explicit terms, he as explicitly disavows that his language implies unrighteousness in God. Rom. ix. 14. It cannot indeed be denied that the mercy of God could have been exercised towards the king of Egypt; but neither can it be claimed that the Divine rectitude demanded the exercise of such mercy. These things are expressly true, that in all his dealings with Pharaoh, God did not tempt him to evil, by exciting evil passions, or infusing evil principles; he did not interfere with the exercise of his free will, or destroy his accountability; but enduring and forbearing with his wilful and stubborn rebellion, he allowed him to go to the utmost limits of human iniquity, as an example to all subsequent ages, that no man can harden his heart against God and prosper. After Pharaoh, who would not fear to harden his heart in sin; after Pharaoh, let every man know the folly and danger of resisting God.

The heart of man is said to be hardened when he is indifferent to those things which ought to interest and impress him. In common language we speak of a man who can commit crimes without remorse as a hardened wretch. When feelings do not rise, which naturally should arise, the heart is hard. This indifference almost invariably springs from long indulged iniquity; so that it is proper for us to say that the hardening of the heart of man is the constant result of instructions despised and duty neglected. It is impossible for any man to know his duty and refuse to do it, without a growing insensibility on his part to its claims upon him. We do not understand that God hardened the heart of Pharaoh by exerting upon him any such power as rendered his mind more obdurate; very certainly, not to affect in any wise the voluntary agency of the wicked king. But as on the one hand he withheld from him those influences of Divine grace which he ever gives according to his own good pleasure; so on the other, he permitted him to choose his own ways of evil, and gave him up to the influence of his own wicked heart. It is worthy of notice that the two expressions "the Lord hardened Pharaoh's heart," ch. x. 27, and Pharaoh hardened his own heart, viii. 32, are both used as meaning the same thing. God is often said to do what he permits to be done; and even the very same thing is, in the Scriptures, ascribed both to Satan and to God. See 2 Sam. xxiv. 1, and 1 Chron. xxi. 1. And it is abundantly plain in the Bible that God threatens to forsake men, if they sin against him; and that when they do not like to retain him in their knowledge, he gives them up to their own ways.

These two lessons every reader of the Bible should learn of Pharaoh.

First. That salvation is of God's free grace. He is bound to none. He has mercy on whom he will have mercy. That ye may know that the Lord doth put a difference between the Egyptians and Israel. This doctrine runs through all the Scriptures. Salvation is of grace. So every man, who desires God's favour, should humbly seek his face Many persons seem to think that if salvation is purely of grace, there is neither need, propriety, nor encouragement to seek God's favour. So the Scriptures do not teach us. They do indeed tell us of men converted to God by free and sovereign grace, when they were careless of him, and never thought of looking for him. God can change a persecuting Saul into a preaching Paul; and can say of many, "I am found of them that sought me not." Isa. lxv. 1. We rejoice in that grace that can so arrest the thoughtless sinner. But it is no less grace, when God gives mercy which sinners seek with tears and prayers. If I help one poor man who does not ask me, and another poor man who does ask me, it may surely be true charity to both! So "God is often found of those that seek him not, but he is always found of those that seek him." How often is the record made, "This poor man cried, and the Lord heard him." Ps. xxxiv. 6.

That salvation is of grace warns us not to offend that God upon whose mercy we are dependent. If dependent upon any man, would you be indifferent whether you pleased or offended him? Nor is it possible for us to appreciate too highly, the warnings and invitations by which God encourages us to seek his grace. Every exhortation to prayer is a proof that his grace may be sought; and that it is none the less grace, when he grants it upon our humble asking. And the grace of God is exercised in such entire consistency with man's nature, that our voluntary powers are addressed; that we are urged to embrace his promises and his service; and that every subject of God's grace is a cheerful and willing subject.

Secondly. How dangerous a thing it is, for any reason, or in any way, to rebel against God. Pharaoh hardened his heart against judgments in which yet were mingled many proofs of God's long-suffering and forbearance. Every token of repentance was followed by the removal of the plagues; and new judgments were sent only upon new evidence of his perverse rebellion. This truth is plain upon all just views of the case, that God dealt in entire righteousness with that proud monarch. We may freely acknowledge that all the doctrinal and practical difficulties, that ever gather about the subject of God's dealings with the sons of men, are found connected with this example. Of these teachings of Moses we may say, as the Apostle Peter says of like teachings in the writings of Paul, "In them are some things hard to be understood." But let us seriously mark what the Apostle adds, that only "the unlearned and unstable wrest" these, and "to their own destruction." 2 Peter iii. 16. Not the legitimate teachings of the Scriptures but the *wresting* of them, and this without a fair understanding of them, injures men. And the end is their own destruction.

But this thought it seems important for every sinful soul to ponder. All the difficulties, objections and cavils that men have ever made against God, his word, or his dealings, only increase the madness of those who dare to rebel against him. When in one of his parables our blessed Lord allows a servant to complain against God as a hard Master, he enters into no vindication; but answers the complainer upon his own terms—"You knew that I was a hard Master. Certainly then you are without excuse for disobeying my *reasonable* commands."

Sinners have nothing to gain by their hostility to God. To neglect his mercies, to defy his judgments, to rebel against his commands, to delay our obedience to him, may not be sins of equal enormity; but they are alike fatal to the soul's immortal interests. However that sad state is reached, it is a dreadful condition when the heart of any man is hardened against God. Let us not be insensible to the voice of his instructions, or to his calls of mercy. It often seems a vain thing to argue against the cavillings which men make respecting things hard to be understood in the Scriptures; not by any means because their objections are unanswerable, or even forcible. But sin darkens the mind and perverts the affections; and truths perfectly plain to a holy mind may be stumbling-blocks to souls that are blinded by prejudice and iniquity. Yet let no sinful man forget—that there rests upon him the imperative, infinite obligation to be reconciled to God; that with whomsoever else he may quarrel, he cannot wisely lay anything to his charge; and that the earliest, the most complete, and the most cheerful submission to all he teaches and to all he requires, is our "beginning of wisdom." What seems darkest is still right; what seems harshest is yet just; while his largest mercies are free; while his words of promise are true; and none have ever trusted in him and been confounded.

CHAPTER XX.

THE PASSOVER INSTITUTED.

"He passed the tents of Jacob o'er,
Nor poured the wrath divine;
He saw the blood on every door
And blessed the peaceful sign." WATTS.

THOUGH Moses was driven forth from the presence of Pharaoh, and though he declares that with Pharaoh's own consent and even urgency, they would soon go forth from the land, the preparations for departure were deliberately made. And before the last plague upon the Egyptians, means are to be used to shield the Israelites from the stroke of the angel; and to impress them with a deep sense of the greatness of their deliverance. The children of Israel were directed to institute the feast long known among them as the feast of the Passover. Four days before the appointed time, they were to select a lamb or a kid, (Ex. xii. 3,) and keep it until the fixed time; and then the Passover must be celebrated.

As this was not a temporary service, nor one of trifling significance in the Jewish church; but one maintained until the opening of the Christian dispensation; continued till now by the scattered remnant of the Jewish people; and even retained in Christian churches under the name of Easter by reason of its connection with the death of Christ, we may give our brief attention to several things pertaining to it.

We may *first* give our thoughts to the Passover, in its services and their immediate design.

The Israelites were commanded to set the lamb apart for this service on the tenth day of the first month; and on the fourteenth day to kill it. This being done, they were to shut themselves up in their abodes, each family by itself, or several smaller families together; to take the blood of the victim, and stain the upper and side posts of the door; to roast the lamb entire with fire; breaking none of the bones; and to remain in the house where they ate it. As it was intended that upon that night they should go forth from the land, so they were to eat this feast in the attitude of preparation. They must stand upon their feet, with their shoes upon them, with their staves in their hands, with their robes girded up about them, and they must eat in haste.

The immediate design of this feast was to impress upon the people that their double deliverance —from the sword of the destroyer, and from the bondage of Egypt—was to be effected by Divine mercy and power. The blood upon the door-posts was doubtless more a sign of their faith than a necessary mark to guide the destroying angel. And yet it seems not hard to understand that the Passover was intended for more important ends than the immediate instruction of the people. It does not seem that the minute directions given for its observance were regarded as obligatory in later times. The sprinkling of the blood upon the door-posts, made no part of the later service. The Saviour and his disciples did not keep the Pass-over, with their loins girded up, nor standing, nor with their staves in their hands; nor did they remain within the house until morning. We cannot decide why the exact form of the original Passover was not retained in the Jewish church, especially in matters that seem so significant; nor can we tell whether the people *gradually* or otherwise, departed from the prescribed rule. That these departures from the letter of the commands originally given, were no serious infringement of Passover law, is evident, since our Lord adopts the practice of his own day, without any word of rebuke upon it, as different from the original institution. The chief design of the service was to remember the deliverance from Egypt by the sprinkling of blood; and to typify by this, the sacrifice of a greater Lamb for a more remarkable deliverance. It is not necessary to judge that the Israelites themselves thoroughly understood the meaning of the service. Indeed the excellence of its testimony to later times may be greater, because the institution possessed a significancy beyond their thoughts; as a prophecy from the lips of a man who does not himself understand it, must have come forth from a wisdom superior to his own.

Perhaps we should *secondly* notice an important historical value that belongs to the Passover.

The entire history of the world does not furnish us with so remarkable a commemorative institution to establish the truth of any historical event, as the Jewish Passover. The deliverance it records, was one so signal in Jewish history, and so witnessed by the entire nation; and so many remarkable things belong to it, and to this commemorative service, that we may regard it as conclusive proof of the genuineness of the entire Mosaic history. It is sometimes compared to the celebration in the United States, of the fourth of July to commemorate the signing of the Declaration of Independence. But if it is impossible that any people could be led to observe such a national festival as the fourth of July, when in fact no such declaration had ever been made; it is much more reasonable to argue that the Passover of the Jews could only arise from the events it professes to keep in memory. This feast sprang not from any later spontaneous movement on the part of the people; but it was authoritatively established at the very time; it was not a holiday for national recreation, but a grave religious festival; it celebrated the birthday of civil and religious liberty among a people whose very existence was perpetuated that they might preserve their religious books and customs; the very dates of their years were changed to make the year thenceforward begin with this important feast; the book in which it is enjoined was written during that generation, and handed down to posterity with the institution it thus commands; and every thing about the ordinance corroborates the facts, which it is designed to commemorate. More than three thousand years have passed away since Moses and the people of Israel kept that feast; and it is still observed, in all their wide dispersion, by the remnant of that scattered race. Manifestly whenever that feast was first instituted, its adoption recognized the Divine authority of Moses. How could the Jewish race ever have been induced to establish such a festival, at the time of the Exodus, or at any subsequent time, unless the events here spoken of really occurred? In the very nature of the human mind, we cannot fail to recognize that an institution like this, fully implies the historical authenticity of the books of Moses, that have been handed down to posterity with this festival.

The Bible is remarkable for three institutions of a commemorative nature, which, apart from their own significance, establish the historical authenticity of the Scriptures. The first historical writer of the Old Testament is Moses; and in his times this Passover feast was enjoined; the last historical book of the Old Testament is that of Esther; and when it was given to the church, the feast Purim was enjoined to commemorate the great deliverance that book records; and with the gospels in the days of our Lord and his apostles, the Lord's Supper was instituted. So that three most important periods of the Scriptural history have similar historical institutions to prove their authenticity;* no ancient writings have testimonials to be compared with these; these testimonials cannot possibly be spurious, nor bear record to a falsehood; and thus the inspired volume has irrefragable proofs of veracity. For if these periods of Scriptural history are confirmed to us, all the rest is necessarily sustained.

But the historical value of the Passover, as bearing testimony to the authenticity of the Mosaic records, is greatly increased, as already suggested, by a species of inherent evidence, which proves the prophetic character of the ordinance. Historical and commemorative, the Passover was, to every age from Moses until now; it was also symbolic and prophetic, beyond the understanding of those who observed this feast until the great day of its fulfilment.

There belongs then *thirdly*, a doctrinal and typical importance to the Passover which we should not overlook.

* See the argument more largely, Esther and her Times, Lect. XII. The world is familiar with Leslie.

Beyond the clear knowledge of the sons of Jacob, the memorial of their deliverance from Egypt gave promise also of a better deliverance, from a more fearful stroke, and by more precious blood. So the Apostle Paul appropriates this ordinance for the instruction of his Christian hearers. "For even Christ our Passover is sacrificed for us." So Christ himself substituted the Lord's Supper for the older ordinance that found its fulfilment in his death. And if we compare the two services we may see that almost every thing in Israel and in the Passover has an answering idea in the sacrifice of Christ.

The bondage of Egypt was as the bondage of sin; the destroying angel is as the sentence of death against every sinful soul; the Paschal lamb typified Christ our atonement; and our only safety is found in the sprinkling of that protecting blood. The Israelites were directed to take of the choicest lambs of their flocks, an unblemished male of the first year: but how excellent is our Lamb, typified in this careful selection. The lamb was to be slain at an appointed time; as Christ Jesus was put to death upon the day of the Passover feast, and in the most public manner. They must put the blood upon the door-posts of their dwellings; as we are saved from the destroyer's sword by the sprinkling of more precious blood. They must be gathered within their abodes and remain there until the danger was past; so we find our refuge by abiding in the church of God, over which alone the destroying angel passes harmlessly. The separation of Israel from Egypt: the safety of the one and the destruction of the other, are significant of the difference which God puts between believers and unbelievers in later times.

We are further taught that we ought to keep the Christian Passover with feelings akin to those which were enjoined upon Israel in their solemn feast. They must search out all the leaven in their houses, and put it away as an emblem of deceit; and we are to keep our feast with the unleavened bread of sincerity and truth. They were to keep the Passover with faith in their covenant God; and our faith too must respect our need of deliverance and his power and grace to save. They must mingle bitter herbs with their eating the Passover; and sorrow and repentance must aid us to keep the feast. Each one among them must partake of the roasted lamb; as we must individually partake of Christ's sacrifice to secure its benefits. And as they sat not down to a quiet meal, but stood as pilgrims ready for a journey; as they took the food hastily, so are we pilgrims going forward; and we partake of a table spread by our Lord in the wilderness that we may have strength to press onward in his service.

It seems not needful now to enlarge upon the practical aspects of the Passover feast. Evidently it was no ordinary institution. With feelings of deep interest and solemnity were the Israelites gathered within their respective dwellings upon that eventful night. It was indeed a night much to be remembered; only comparable in the history of man to that darker and more

> "Dreadful night,
> When powers of earth and hell arose
> Against the Son of God's delight,
> And friends betrayed him to his foes."

It is an interesting thing to notice that the Passover is in this, like all the important teachings of the Jewish church; like the Old Testament itself, only of greater importance and interest and instruction to the Christian church than it was to the Jewish. Their experience in piety was like ours in every important feature; but we have clearer light and higher privileges. We see clearly what they saw darkly; and the great things that happened unto them are for our learning.

CHAPTER XXI.

THE DEATH OF THE FIRST-BORN.

"Then rose a cry, and every mother wept
Over the cradle where her first-born slept."

We have sufficiently considered the plagues of Egypt to realize that they were deeply distressing. Yet up to this period, we have no record of the actual loss of any human life among that people. But this next great grief now laid upon them for their perverse rebellion against God, is perhaps the most severe that is recorded in all the history of man, as borne by any nation. The loss of their army, and perhaps their king at its head, in the Red Sea, was a calamity less appalling, and one that would be less sensibly felt, than the destruction of their first-born.

When an army is enlisted for war and goes forth to battle, everybody understands that each individual of that army, from the meanest soldier to the chief commander, is exposed to a sudden and violent death. However weak the opposing forces may be, or however easy may be the victory over them, still, any one of these warriors, going forth in his strength, may never return. Such a liability hangs over every one. It was a terrible disaster to Egypt when their entire army perished in the waters of the Red Sea. Yet whole armies have been lost, on various occasions; and neither this nor the severest battles can affect directly every family of a nation. All the differences between a soldier and a citizen; war and peace; a partial and a universal calamity, may be marked between the destruction in the Red Sea, and the smiting of Egypt's first-born by the destroying angel.

The excellencies of home include love and peace, happiness and security. It is true indeed that this household, gathered beneath one roof and bound together in bonds of sacred affection, is not exempt from care and anxiety. Disease often enters the happiest homes; death separates our loved ones from us. But when these sorrows come, there are many alleviations. The sympathies of friends gather around the afflicted household to sustain them in their trials; and kindly affection is grateful to the troubled mind. But in this fearful hour in Egypt, each house is necessarily occupied with its own trouble. The palaces of the royal and the noble, the cottage of the peasant, the hut of the beggar and the slave, are open alike to that sword of avenging wrath. What a variety too of age and influence belonged to that description, "the first-born in every house."

How much of affliction belonged to the sudden work and the mysterious nature of this visitation. Perhaps indeed a few of the servants of Pharaoh knew the declaration of the Hebrew prophets; knew that their words would surely come to pass; and were filled with painful apprehensions as they looked upon their first-born; and knew no means of averting the coming danger. But to almost all, the trouble came unlooked for. The household separated at night for their usual quiet and secure slumbers. And if at the midnight hour the mother had been aroused by the moaning of an unquiet sleeper in the cradle beside her; if the parents had found the burning of a fever, or the incoherence of delirium in the restless tossings of a beloved one, their alarm and anxiety would be less, to recognize in these the symptoms of some familiar disease. We do not know by what means the Lord's messenger to Egypt performed his errand. Yet doubtless that unknown midnight plague and in every household, was beyond description terrible.

And as the usual call for the aid and sympathy of neighbours made known the dreadful truth that every house was the scene of a similar calamity; when wailings met the ear from every dwelling, of the aged over the stay of their declining years, of the young mother over her darling, and of the young wife over her cold husband; when they recalled the fearful judgments that had of late distressed their land; and when the present distress, superior to all the rest, is referred to the struggle between Pharaoh and Moses, it is no wonder that with one common impulse, the Egyptians were urgent for the departure of Israel.

We know not by what agency this fearful destruction was wrought. A single, created angel could not, as we may suppose, visit every Egyptian dwelling at a single hour of the night. But truly, whatever does the Lord's will, is the Lord's angel. He makes the winds his messengers and the lightnings his servants. Perhaps these reasons for forbidding the Israelites to leave their dwellings until the morning may be suggested; that it might be evident that this destruction came by no agency of theirs, and that they might all be assembled ready for their departure from the land.

Many discussions have been held upon the statement that the Israelites at the command of God *borrowed* from the Egyptians jewels of gold and silver; and took these with them as they left the land. Some have argued that this was but a robbery upon their part, and this the worse because they were divinely ordered to do this. Suffice it for us to make two remarks upon the matter.

1st. The brevity of these records often leaves us ignorant of many circumstances which might fully explain any obscure points. That any thing contrary to rectitude was enjoined upon Israel, we have no reason to believe.

2d. Many scholars allege that the word here used is not the ordinary word for borrow. See Deut. xxviii. 12, Neh. v. 4: לוה. This word is rather the ordinary word for "ask" or "demand." A demand was made upon the Egyptians, which in their peculiar circumstances they felt no disposition to refuse. The bondage of Israel had been oppressive, and the Egyptians had long enough reaped the fruits of their unrequited toils. It may therefore have been but distributive justice to render these returns. And though the king of Egypt had so hardened his heart, yet the people greatly feared the Israelites because of the judgments of their God; and this even before the destruction of their first-born; much more after that. To all this it may be added, that in such contests between two nations, as this between Egypt and Israel, as indeed in all warfare, the power of spoiling their enemies has ever been exercised by the victors. The Israelites carried off the spoils of Egypt; not secured by guile or treachery, but openly demanded of them; and their rightful due by reason of many years of toil. Nor should we forget the promise long before made by God to Abraham that after their servitude in a strange land his children should come out with great substance. Gen. xv. 14.

The going forth of Israel from Egypt is so briefly and simply stated in the narrative of Moses that few persons ever realize how great a thing it was. The world never saw, before or since, such an emigration. Here were six hundred thousand men going forth in one vast company together with their women and children and cattle. It does not seem needful to claim that these men were all capable of bearing arms; yet the entire number would scarcely be less than two millions. We cannot think it possible, that these numbers could be brought together, and led forth from Egypt in one night. It seems much more likely that the seven days after the Passover, during which they must eat unleavened bread, was spent in gathering to Etham by the edge of the wilderness. The time is not noted in the narrative; but at the end of a month from the Passover, the hosts had only gone three or four days' journey beyond the Red Sea. Ex. xv. 22: xvi. 1. It may be that full two weeks passed, from the destruction of the first-born to the passage of the Sea; and even in this time so large a body could not have been gathered to a single place of rendezvous, but for the guidance of that remarkable Pillar by which God himself led them forth. It was an easy thing for vast bodies of them to gather together, even by separate divisions, when such an appearance taught them where to go. The narrative says, the children of Israel went up *harnessed;* i. e. in military order; as the margin says, "five in a rank." But it may mean in five separate bodies, which perhaps came together at Raamses. But it is certainly appropriate to say that Israel went forth with a *high hand.*

But doubtless the hurry and excitement was greatest, both among the Israelites and the Egyptians, upon that memorable night. The anguish of Egypt dare not find its expression in vengeance upon Israel. Even Pharaoh, now at last brought to urge them to go forth, beseeches them to bless him by asking for him the favour of their awful God; and all the people of the land, only too glad to see them go, are ready to afford them all the aid in their power. As God threatened that he would specially execute judgment upon the Egyptian gods upon that night, Ex. xii. 12, it may be that they found their idols fallen, as afterwards Dagon fell before the Ark of the Lord, 1 Sam. v. 3; or perhaps the animals kept for worship died; and this added to the distress of the Egyptians. The children of Israel therefore went forth, not only unopposed, but even aided by the Egyptians.

It would also seem that in the excitement of that wonderful march, many of the Egyptians joined themselves to Israel, and went forth with their advancing hosts. These are called by Moses a "mixed multitude." They were, if we may judge from the subsequent history, of no advantage to Israel. See Numb. xi. 4. They were doubtless the fickle populace, perhaps from the lower classes in the Egyptian cities, ready to be carried away by any tide of excitement. They joined themselves to the advancing hosts of God's people, from no understanding of the principles of piety in Israel; and from no true attachment to Israel's God. Such a multitude could only be a hindrance to the hosts. They were all idolaters; and though it may be that some of them learned lessons of saving wisdom as they dwelt in the tents of God's people, it is most likely that the chief part of them found their graves in the wanderings of the desert, among those that provoked God by their murmurings.

If it seems strange to us that such a rabble would be allowed to go forth in the Exodus of Israel, let us remember that an entire separation between God's chosen people and the unbelieving world has never been effected upon earth. Usually the church is in the world; and even in the deserts of Sinai, Israel was not alone. All were not Israel which were of Israel, Rom. ix. 6; and a mixed company of idolaters was around them and among them. So now Christ pleads, "I pray not that thou shouldest take them out of the world." John xvii. 15.

CHAPTER XXII.

ISRAEL AT THE RED SEA.

"The man of God
O'er the wide waters lifts his mighty rod,
And onward treads. The circling waves retreat
In hoarse deep murmurs, from his holy feet;
And the chased surges, inly roaring, show
The hard wet sand and coral hills below." HEBER.

THE children of Israel now began their long-designed march from Egypt. But God's thoughts are not man's thoughts. Their first steps toward liberty seem to bring them into new difficulties. Their nearest route to Canaan would have led them northward, along the coast of the Mediterranean Sea; but instead of pursuing this, or even instead of turning around the head of the Red Sea to leave Egypt as speedily as possible, they took what seemed to be the worst possible route. They turned down the western side of the Red Sea; and seemed to march away from the Isthmus of Suez, by which alone they could reach Asia from Africa.

And yet there was in this, only a seeming mistake; for they were under Divine direction. The wonderful Pillar by which God designed to lead their way, which seemed but a cloud in the sky by day, but which at night grew luminous, was their ever visible guide. Led by this Pillar, they were in the right way; though often they themselves may have feared they were not. Many among them were doubtless entirely ignorant of the geography of the country, and of the true route to Canaan; but if a few of the Israelites, or of the Egyptian camp followers, knew the true route they could easily excite uneasiness and murmuring against their leaders.

There are three reasons, apparent to us, for the circuitous and unwonted route of the Israelites as they went forth from Egypt.

First. God thus showed his kindness to the people in sparing them from the attacks of enemies, they were not as yet prepared to meet. The nearest road led through the warlike tribes of the Philistines. But the sons of Jacob, having been so long oppressed in Egypt, had nothing either of the spirit of freemen, or of the experience needful to contend with those who are inured to arms. Ex. xiii. 17, 18. They are not allowed to meet trials for which they have as yet no preparation. We often think our present trials hard to bear; and yet they may even be sent in God's mercy, to save us from other troubles that are really beyond our strength. This change of their route may have been a great trial of the faith of Moses. For if we suppose that in his earlier years, he had possessed experience in leading armies, we must believe that he was not ignorant of the ordinary route. He would naturally make full inquiries before undertaking to lead out this great multitude; and indeed he had himself twice gone over the route from Egypt to Sinai, in addition to the knowledge of the Red Sea, which he may have gained from forty years' residence in Arabia. No man in all the camp better understood what a false movement was made by turning down the western side of the Red Sea. And yet Moses did not hesitate to surrender his own judgment, and to march quietly forward, where Divine guidance evidently led.

Secondly. God led his people out of the usual road to Canaan that they might secure a final illustrious triumph over their enemies. It is plain that Pharaoh had let the people go only because he could no longer keep them; and that his heart was as hostile to them and to their God as ever. And now after a few days had given him time to recover the dreadful shock of the loss of their first-born; and when new thirstings for vengeance took the place of grief; when the king of Egypt learned that the Israelites had taken the wrong road, he may have thought that this itself was a proof that God was not their guide. Perhaps he might reason, that if God was their guide, they would at least have known that they were quite out of the proper road; and the very fact that they were so, gave him encouragement that his armies could reduce them to subjection, and lead them back again to Egypt. But only by false reasoning does either friend or foe argue that God has forsaken his people. Better for Pharaoh had he learned the lessons already given, and known by experience, at least thus late, that, "No weapon formed against Zion shall prosper."

Thirdly. God led his people thus far out of the natural way to Canaan to teach them and us, a lesson of spiritual progress; and to lead them to the exercise of faith. The way round about is the right way, if for nothing else, because it bids us trust in his guidance and calls forth our faith. They were led into perplexity; indeed into such perplexity as forbade any solution, except as they reposed their confidence in God. Every guide they could consult, who had any experience of the routes, or any knowledge of the geography of the country, would assure them that they were wrong; and that they could find no outlet to the desert by marching to the south. Yet they had sufficient proof that they were right, since they had followed the guidance of the great Pillar. This was not the first time that God had led them through trouble on their way to relief; and he had shown his power to save before, when they could not anticipate how he would work. And surely a people who had so recently known the mighty hand of God for their defence and deliverance, should have been willing now to trust him, without the sight of their eyes.

Faith ought to have said, that some good reason, for his glory and Israel's good, had brought them by this unaccustomed route.

The precise point to which the hosts of Israel passed down the western coast of the Red Sea and then passed through its divided waters, is a matter not now easy to settle. In fact we may esteem this one of the most difficult questions of Biblical geography. The difficulty arises in part from the brevity of the narrative; and in part from changes that have taken place in the sea itself. It is evident from the reports of travellers that that remarkable body of water is not now so large as formerly. Dr. Robinson, who made his observations along the coast for the express purpose of determining where the passage of the children of Israel took place, supposes that it was near Suez, not far from what is now the head of the Red Sea. Others suppose that the crossing took place ten or twelve miles lower down. If, with Dr. Robinson, we regard the place as at Suez, we find there a plain capable of holding two millions of men with the mountains approaching so close to the sea, that but a narrow defile remains along the shore.* Such a place as this would fully meet the words of Pharaoh, "they are entangled in the land." This point of the Red Sea can now be crossed as a ford; and it is worthy of our notice that Napoleon Buonaparte and his staff crossed it in 1799; and mis-

* Kurtz's Old Cov., ii. 374.

taking the route, and darkness coming on, they were exposed to imminent danger, and were rescued only by his capacity and presence of mind.* But even now *caravans* never cross this ford; while there is proof enough that formerly this part of the sea was both wider and deeper.†

If we are to understand that the children of Israel advanced through an open valley until they were hemmed in, by the mountains and the sea; and that then the army of Pharaoh was able to take possession of their only way of retreat, we need not wonder that their passage through the waters is recorded as a triumph of faith. The king of Egypt, learning the route they had taken, thought he was sure of them. They were forsaken of God, or they would not be there. They were unable to fight his armies, and as unable to flee. The king assembled as much of an army as he could within a brief space. And this was by no means inconsiderable. For warriors were ranked as a distinct and highly honourable class in Egypt; and a large standing army was maintained. The army of Sesostris according to Diodorus was 600,000 infantry, 24,000 cavalry, and 27,000 war chariots. Josephus says that at this time, Pharaoh led out 600 chariots, 50,000 horse-

* Alison's Europe, i. 518.

† Robinson, i. 85. Kitto Sc. Lands, 57. Yet Bonar says, "The shoals all run up and down the gulf, not *across* it." Desert of Sinai, 92.

men, and 200,000 footmen. But the narrative in Exodus mentions only chariots and cavalry: (compare xiv. 9, 23, xv. 1.) Pharaoh took six hundred picked chariots and all his other chariots. Perhaps only the cavalry and chariots were taken because the pursuit was made in haste. The Egyptians were anciently very famous for their horses; and upon the monuments, war chariots are frequently found. Sometimes a chariot carries two men, one to fight, and the other to drive; and sometimes there are three men, the third being the armour-bearer, or sometimes two of them are warriors.*

Many writers upon this portion of the history seem to take it for granted that all these events occurred within three or four days of the keeping of the Passover. But the narrative gives no data upon which to determine this. A month intervened between the slaying of the first-born in Egypt and the arrival of the Israelites in the wilderness of Sin, three days' journey, or a little more, from the Red Sea. Ex. xv. 22, xvi. 1. We may therefore, without violating the narrative, suppose that the movements of the Egyptians were more deliberate. A few days spent in recovering from the dreadful stroke so lately felt, and in forming their purposes of vengeance, when they

* Kurtz, ii. 354. Wilkinson, i. 368. Rollin, i. 120. It is said that the ancient Egyptians used no cavalry. Yet this cannot be certainly affirmed. See Smith's Dict. Bible, ii. 1017.

heard that the Israelites were apparently in their power, would seem at least natural in their circumstances. But having once made up their minds that they had acted foolishly in letting their bondmen go, and that now they could retrieve the error, no doubt the actual pursuit was rapid. The first knowledge the Israelites had of the matter was the sight of the hosts of Pharaoh, which they could not resist, taking possession of the defile behind them, so that also they could not fly.

It is no matter of surprise that consternation and distress spread through the hosts of Israel, as it became speedily known that Pharaoh was behind them. If the Divine guidance had prevented them from marching through the territories of the Philistines, because the people were unprepared for war, they were surely not prepared now to fight with these well trained Egyptian warriors. That these were their old oppressors, from whose tyranny they had no spirit to free themselves, would make them more afraid. And indeed we do not know that the Israelites were at this time possessed of any weapons of warfare. Rather we conclude that, as a mass, they were an unarmed multitude. They may have added to the few arms already in their hands, by the spoils of these very enemies, washed up for them from the depths of the sea; and the skilful men who afterwards made the tabernacle may have taught the people to make themselves arms before they came into actual warfare with any enemies. But we cannot be surprised that the people were greatly distressed when they saw the Egyptian army. They ought indeed to have borne in mind the manifold deliverances that God had already wrought within the past few months of their history. How could they forget, that Pharaoh's rage brought only severer judgments against himself and larger mercies to Israel? And yet this is our poor sinful nature. Every new trial drives away the remembrance of past mercies; and we easily deem ourselves forsaken of God. But the Israelites went much farther than this. As when heavier burdens had been laid upon them, (v. 21,) so now, they murmured against Moses; and complained that he brought them away from the ease of Egypt to find graves in the desert.

CHAPTER XXIII.

RED SEA LESSONS.

"Sound the loud timbrel o'er Egypt's dark sea,
Jehovah has triumphed! His people are free!
Sing! for the pride of the tyrant is broken;
His chariots, his horsemen all splendid and brave,
How vain was their boasting! The Lord has but spoken
And chariots and horsemen are sunk in the wave!
Sound the loud timbrel o'er Egypt's dark sea!
Jehovah has triumphed! His people are free!"

THE position occupied by Moses at this time, remarkably exemplifies the meekness and the faith of the man of God. No one in all the camp was better aware than himself of the difficulties around them; indeed he would not have led the hosts in this direction, but for the manifest leadings of Divine providence. And because he was a believer, this was his comfort and support that he had not brought these difficulties upon himself. This was his confidence, that if Divine wisdom had led him into straits, Divine mercy and Divine power would open a way out. Perhaps even Moses did not as yet know how this deliverance would be effected. The opening of the sea may have as little entered his thoughts as the thoughts of rebellious Israel, or even of hardened Pharaoh. But we may well agree to call Moses a man of preëminent meekness, when the ingratitude and injustice of Israel towards himself, and their provocation against God, did not move him to indignation. The people ought to have remembered what their great leader had done for them. No man in that vast congregation had taken a deeper interest in their welfare than he had. None of them had sacrificed more than he; none had more exposed themselves to the indignation of Pharaoh; none had more to fear from the success of the Egyptians.*

But Moses stood calm and forbearing, while the camp was filled with the utmost agitation. He made no effort to vindicate himself; but he attempted to quiet the Israelites by assuring them that they had no occasion to fear; nor need they lift a hand to resist or to smite Egypt. By the Lord's power they should be delivered; and they now looked on these dreaded foes for the last time. Yet this seems to have been a time on the part of Moses of earnest prayer to God. It is not recorded that he uttered any prayer in the sight of the people. Perhaps it was in the depths of his own heart, deeply affected by their perilous position, yet relying upon the power of God, that his prayer went up for the needed deliverance.

* Bush.

But the time has now come for action; and with this, prayer must not be allowed to interfere. Sometimes God's people can do nothing, but pray; and then they should pray; and while praying, stand still and see the salvation of God. But the truly devout mind stands still neither through indolence nor presumption: it is ready to act as soon as the time comes for proper action; and thus praying, and waiting and acting may be but different workings of the same faith, as circumstances may bid us do one or the other. That all the glory of this great deliverance may be given to God alone, Moses is simply to lift his rod over the waters, and Divine power must open the pathway through the sea.

And now first the command goes through the camp of the Israelites that they must prepare to march. The order is deliberate, yet preparation in so vast a host is no slight matter. Perhaps this was just about evening; and the Egyptians, sure of their prey, had made arrangements for the night's repose, after their fatiguing march. Doubtless they were ignorant of the stir in the camp of Israel. For we have some just reason to think that the passage of the children of Israel through the Red Sea was attended by such a tremendous storm, such an agitation of the earth, the air, and the seas; the earth quaking, the rain dashing, the winds howling, the lightning flashing, the thunder pealing, the waves roaring; as mortal man had never before seen these things. That the people went through dry shod, refers only to their safe passage, i. e. through the waters of the sea; but it does not affirm that no rain fell upon them from above. Rather every word of this description corresponds with the words of a Psalmist, who expressly tells us how the people passed through the Red Sea. He says the sea was afraid: "the depths also were troubled; the clouds poured out water; the skies sent out a sound; thine arrows also went abroad; the voice of thy thunder was in the heaven; thy lightnings lightened the world; the earth trembled and shook," Ps. lxxvii. 16—20, when God led his people like a flock by the hand of Moses and Aaron.

The next movement, after the orders issued by Moses, was the removal of the guiding Pillar, which now in the sight of all Israel became their protecting rear-guard. God is either before or behind his people, according as their necessities demand; before to lead them in unknown ways, behind to guard them from pursuing foes. To the Egyptians perhaps this cloud of awful blackness was the apparent cause of the storm then raging; and the movements of the Israelites were more easily made because their enemies thought that no army could march at such a time. But the cloud that was dark to them, was light all night to Israel. And when all was ready and the lawgiver gave the command to go forward, it was by faith that Israel passed through the sea. Marshalled in wide ranks that the passage might be more speedy, perhaps the waters still dashed upon the shore in rising fury, until the feet of the foremost were almost dipped in the surf; and to advance seemed an act of madness, rather than of faith. Yet this was the way in which the Divine word bade them go, and they went forward. And as they went, what a deliverance took place! The waves of the sea parted; the waters ranged themselves on either hand; the path was open. In one sense, this was no great thing for God to do. Every day of the world's history, he does far more stupendous things by his ordinary working. Every day the entire waters of the ocean are lifted up from their bed and sent back again by mighty power; yet nobody wonders at the tides, because they regularly occur. Want of power, or want of means to effect this wonder at the Red Sea, surely could not hinder its occurrence.. In another sense, this was a great thing for God to do. Chiefly let us recognize that to show forth his own glory, and his readiness to bless his people, "he did marvellous things at the Red Sea." Egypt for perverse rebellion deserved this judgment; the tribes around needed some public demonstration of his power that should strike them with a wholesome terror for the protection of Israel, Ex. xv. 14, 15; and Israel would naturally have more confidence in their protecting God.

And Moses stretched out his hand over the sea, and not without the action of the wind upon the waters, the waves parted, and a path was made for the advancing hosts. This was indeed a wonderful scene; and we cannot imagine the emotions of the people as they followed their intrepid leader. The severity of the storm around them, the strange bulwarks of restless waters held in restraint on either side, and the bright shining of that glorious cloud, which not only gave them light to go, but gave them also Divine assurance of safety, would impress them with a serious awe, almost in contrast with the emotions of hope and joy and gratitude which sprang from their deliverance. But doubtless the thoughts of the Israelites were almost as various as the numbers of the people. How many passed through the Red Sea with bold and unfaltering step, with faith in their hearts and songs upon their lips; and how many that fearful night, pale with terror, were but hastened forward as others bore them, like light and lifeless straws upon a hurrying current; how many perhaps even then longed for Egypt, when thus passing forward to Canaan. Even a Red Sea's deliverance was no proof of spiritual faith. Rejoice not if the waves obey you, or if the devils are subject to you; but rather rejoice that your names are written in heaven. The miracles of those days did not lift them above us. We have teachings of truth and calls of grace at least as clear as any they had; and salvation belongs not specially to days of miracles. An apostle expressly instructs us that with many who passed through that baptism in the Red Sea, God was not well pleased; for they were afterwards overthrown in the wilderness. 1 Cor. x. 1—5.

When the Egyptians learned that the Israelites had nearly passed the Red Sea, they pressed on in pursuit. They even dared to pass in between those tremendous walls, and to seek their revenge in the bed of the sea. Apparently forgetting that ten times already had the Lord put a difference between his foes and his friends, with the sound of trumpets, the rush of chariots and the clang of arms, they hurried on. And not until they had advanced too far to admit of retreat, did they discover the hostile aspect of the separating cloud. Never before had an army been in such a place; the moist sea-weed, or the yielding sand beneath them; the glassy wall of threatening waters on either hand; and above them, not only the war of the elements, but the flashing fires of that awful Pillar. What a panic was that in the Egyptian ranks when the cry arose, "Let us flee, for the Lord fighteth for Israel." Ex. xiv. 25. Unhappy people! that they had not thought of the Lord before! But the rear-rank, that could not learn so soon the causes for dismay, pressed still forward, and all efforts to retreat only increased the confusion. And just at the dreadful moment of their greatest alarm; when the light shone at last to reveal the surrounding perils; when broken chariots and maddened horses and bewildered men entangled each other in inextricable confusion, the Hebrew prophet stretched forth his rod over the sea. What is man to contend against his God? What can a city do when fire kindles upon its palaces, and a devouring conflagration leaps wildly from square to square? What can a people do when the very air we breathe puts forth its latent energies in the resistless sweep of the hurricane? What are weapons of war, what are human efforts, before the mighty rush of billows? The sea covered Pharaoh, his chosen captains, and his chariots; they sank like lead in the mighty waters.

With deep gratitude to God the Israelites led on by Miriam, the sister of Moses and Aaron, sang a song of triumph on the shore of the Red Sea. She it was, who fourscore years ago had stood as a timid watcher by the reedy border of the Nile, that her infant brother might find needful protection; and she deems herself not too old now to lead forth the daughters of her people with the timbrel and in dances, to praise the name of their delivering God. This triumph by the Red Sea is in part the fruit of Miriam's watchings over her infant brother. How many links go to form the chain of providence for the deliverance of God's people; how little can we afford to lose the slightest of them; and how long it may be, before we can discern the connection of things like these,* Miriam's watchings by the river, Miriam's triumph by the sea.

The lessons of the Red Sea, in how many things may they instruct and console, and animate us. When our souls are not led in the nearest way to Canaan; when the leadings of Providence seem themselves to err; when we are entangled in the wilderness and no path of relief is open; when perplexities increase rather than disperse, and matters grow worse rather than better; when our enemies begirt us round with threatenings never before uttered, let us remember Israel at the Red Sea; let us cry unto God as did Moses; let us move forward at his command.

No lesson is more important for the instruction of those that put their trust in the God of Israel than this: that the deliverance at the Red Sea was wrought by Divine intervention. And every intelligent man, who reads devoutly the history of our race or who studies wisely his own individual experience, can recall instances where great blessings have been secured, imminent perils averted, and signal deliverances given, which could not justly be ascribed to the power or wisdom of the human actors. God rules in the affairs of men by providence, as truly and often quite

* Women of the Old and New Testament.

as remarkably, as in the days of miracle. These interventions are not so given as to hinder human duty; but rather so as to lead men to acknowledge and to rely upon that Divine Power which can make the right successful against the most numerous foes; and to remind us that nothing is more needful or more reasonable than the humble cry of distress in the ear of a delivering God.

The perplexities of Abraham on Moriah, Gen. xxii. 1—10; the perplexities of Joseph in Potiphar's house, Gen. xxxix. 9; of Esther venturing before Ahasuerus, Esther v. 2; of the paralytic bidden to rise and walk, Matt. ix. 6; of the man bidden to stretch forth his hand, Matt. xii. 13, teach us Red Sea lessons. Go forward; do as God bids; for God sustains.

And the Red Sea lesson of triumph may remind us of a greater triumph. We join the swelling anthem,

"Sound the loud timbrel o'er Egypt's dark sea,
Jehovah has triumphed! His people are free!"

But the song of Moses at the Red Sea, but reminds us of a greater triumph and a nobler song,—the song of Moses and of the Lamb, Rev. xv. 3. When the church has gained her last victory; not with the wilderness before, but with all dangers past; not on the shore of the Red Sea, but on the sea of glass; not on earth but in heaven, well may the triumphal song be raised. The victory will be due to the Lamb; and their song will be in his praise.

Happy day for the friends of God! Alas for his foes in that hour of final triumph to Israel!

CHAPTER XXIV.

PROVIDENCE IN THE DESERT.

"When Israel of the Lord beloved,
  Out of the land of bondage came,
Her fathers' God before her moved,
  An awful guide, in smoke and flame;
By day along the astonished lands
  The cloudy pillar glided slow;
By night Arabia's crimsoned sands
  Returned the fiery pillar's glow." SCOTT.

IN the history of the Israelites as recorded by Moses, and in the commission of Moses himself, there is a strange mingling of two things, which men are prone to think quite discordant. These two things are divine and human agency employed to effect just the same things. We find these apparently as distinct as possible. The people seem left to do for themselves just as if God neither provided, nor helped; and yet the divine relief comes as they need it, and beyond their power to aid themselves. We find these things even in cases where we would not look for them; as when Moses, though a prophet of God, seems to receive instruction in matters that pertain to the rule of God's house, not only from human wisdom and experience, but from a man not numbered among the favoured people of God. Men are prone to think, that if God instructs his people, they do not need to consult human wisdom at all; that especially inspiration precludes all dependence upon what men may think; and that a time of miraculous interventions is a time when neither our hearts nor our hands need to be employed.

But see this matter illustrated by two examples, both occurring between the Red Sea and Sinai. That people led forth by the Pillar of Divine guidance must march three days' journey in the wilderness without water. Men who have never been twenty-four hours thirsting in all their lives, can form but a faint idea of the sufferings that come upon the human frame for a short time deprived of water. Doubtless the Israelites had carried some water with them, but a supply totally inadequate; and three days of thirst, to a vast multitude like this, must have produced great distress. And even when they came to water, this distress was heightened by finding that it was bitter.

It is thought that Marah and Elim can both be recognized at the present day. The Arabs regard the water as the worst along the coast;* but its bad qualities vary with different times of the year. Camels however will drink the water; and perhaps it appeared worse to the Israelites, because they had been all their lives accustomed to the excellent

* Kitto's Daily Illustrations.

water of the Nile. How great the disappointment of the thirsty multitude to find water that was unfit to drink! But their consolation must come from Divine power. At the prayer of Moses, the Lord showed a tree, which being cast into the water healed its bitterness. Search has been made in the desert for some tree or shrub, having medical properties equal to the correcting of the waters, but we have no reason to judge that this healing was through the natural virtue of any wood.

After thirst comes hunger. The people passed on from their encampment at Elim; but their supplies of food began to fail. Doubtless they carried with them but a small store of provisions; and their flocks and herds may have been the private property of comparatively but a few persons in the camp. A new series of murmurings therefore began against their great leaders. They complained that they had not been left in Egypt; but had been brought away from a land of plenty to perish in the wilderness. In answer to their necessities the Lord declared by Moses how he would provide food for them in the desert. Two kinds of food were provided for them.

First. There was a supply of quails brought into the camp upon which the people fed. There is a species of quail, "about the size of a turtle-dove," found now in those regions. If they came in any such flocks as the wild pigeons of our western continent, we can easily understand that the entire congregation would be supplied. This bird is often fatigued by its long flight in crossing the waters, and flies so low as to become an easy prey. We are not led to believe that this supply of food was permanent. We read, a year afterwards, of a similar flight of birds upon the camp, Numb. xi. 31, but doubtless the quails now sent afforded food to the congregation for but a few days.

Secondly. A more permanent and abundant supply of food was given in the manna that now fell around the camp, and was granted to the wandering people from this time forward, until they passed beyond the bounds of the desert and entered the land of Canaan.

We do not know the qualities or taste of this food, miraculously provided for Israel in their journeys. We have no reason to believe that it resembled at all, what we now call manna; or that the gum now gathered from the shrubs in that wilderness is at all like it. Modern mannas are condiments or medicinal; the manna of the wilderness was nutritious, and used for food. The people had never seen the like of this before; and when they saw it, they said one to another, Manhu? What is this? Hence the name Manna. Moses told them it was the bread by which God would support them. Its appearance was as small globules, like the hoar-frost, or "coriander seed;" its colour, the colour of bdellium, i. e. a yellowish white, Numb. xi. 7; its taste is doubly described as like cakes slightly sweetened with honey; and as like fresh oil. Ex. xvi. 31, Num. xi. 8. The mode of preparing it may have varied the taste.

If disposed to wonder at the supply of food thus furnished in the pathless wilderness for the sustenance of so large a body of people, surely we need not doubt that Divine power could thus meet their daily need. For, every day of the world's history, immensely larger bounties are scattered through all the earth by the liberality of the God of providence. Year after year, century after century since he created the world, has God given his sun to shine on the evil and on the good, and sent his rain on the just and the unjust. Not one single day has ever failed of his care towards the children of men. Famines have indeed come, harvests have failed, want has been felt; as the Israelites hungered and thirsted in the desert, that man may learn whence his blessings come. Yet in an important sense, not a day has ever passed without God's providential supplies in all the earth, to which every exception has been slight and partial.

And who can reckon the vast supply that is necessary for the food of a single day in all the earth? How much does one great city consume in a single day? How much this entire land? How much populous China? How much all the men in the world? How much the cattle? How much all the living beings in the earth and sea? It is no slight thing to say, "These all wait upon him, and he gives them their meat in due season." And as the manna lay upon the ground, so out of the earth ultimately, all living things are fed. And as the manna fell morning by morning, so vast multitudes upon the earth know not with each rising morning, whence their daily bread must come. Every day the God of providence does greater things than feed the nation of Israël. The miracle of the manna is worthy of our admiration not so much for its magnitude, as for its instructive teachings.

The manna in the wilderness was not simply a miracle, but a combination of miracles. *That* it fell regularly every morning; *that* the quantity that fell and even that which each man gathered was neither in defect nor excess; *that* the supply was regularly cut off upon the Sabbath when it was unlawful to gather it; *that* twice the usual quantity regularly fell upon the day before the Sabbath; *that* it would keep sweet over the Sabbath, and not over any other day; *that* a small portion, laid up in the ark for a testimony, kept for several hundred years, until destroyed in the burning of Solomon's temple; and *that* after supplying them forty years, the manna ceased the very day they ceased to need it: all these are remarkable matters.

And evidently the Sabbath was a religious and familiar ordinance before the law was given on Sinai. It is no disproof of this, that some of the people thought to gather manna on the Sabbath. These may have been irreligious persons, who knew, but disregarded the law; or of the "mixed multitude," who knew it not; or Israelites who in the bondage were forced to labour upon the Sabbath. But at the most, they were exceptions; and even they knew enough to justify the indignation of Moses for their Sabbath-breaking. But here is plain proof afforded that the Sabbath is a religious institution, dating back to the beginning, and not finding its origin at Sinai; a law for the race, and in no just sense a merely Jewish law; and essentially requiring rest from ordinary labour. And the Divine regard for the Sabbath, and the Divine care that man should not labour upon this holy day, are seen in the remarkable fact "that three miracles were wrought every week in special honour of the Sabbath: double the quantity fell the day before; none fell on the Sabbath-day; nor did that corrupt which they kept for that day."*

We may easily know the design of these Divine teachings. The children of Israel were allowed to suffer thirst and hunger until distress invaded their camp, before the Lord afforded them relief. The Israelites were under Divine teachings; they were scholars learning lessons of Divine wisdom; and we are chiefly to regard the tendencies of their experience. Every wise teacher aims to call forth the capacities of the pupil. He therefore

* Scott.

will not solve for him his hard problems; he wishes him to solve them; and this not for the value of the solution, but for the knowledge and skill thereby acquired. God did not design merely to feed his people in the desert. Had this alone been his purpose, they would never have known a want from the Red Sea to the Jordan. But he expressly declares that he led them forty years through the wilderness to humble them, to prove them, to try their hearts; he suffered them to hunger that they might know that man truly lives by every word that proceeds from the mouth of the Lord. Deut. viii. 2, 3. The life of man is not the mere keeping together of this soul and this body. No man has a true appreciation of his own life, who is not ready to die, rather than to do many things. Indeed that only is a true life that is subject in all things to the authority of God. Spiritual life is the true life of man. Whatever promotes this is chiefly valuable to us.

When our Lord Jesus Christ in the time of his temptation in the wilderness, suffered the pangs of hunger, and Satan attempted to lead him to do that which in his estate of humiliation was equivalent to a distrust of God's providence, he replied by quoting these words of Moses, "Man doth not live by bread alone." And this is not only the lesson of Israel's wanderings in the wilderness of Sinai, but the lesson of all the Bible; and the lesson we are constantly taught by the dispensations of God's providence. God fed the people by the daily manna; he gave them water from the flinty rock; he preserved their garments from waxing old in their marches; yet hunger and thirst and anxiety were sent upon them; and the faith of some and the distrust of others were called forth. And thus he deals with us. Whether we have lived twenty years, or forty, or sixty, our daily food has not been lacking; and yet care and toil and anxiety have been our lot. God has so managed our affairs as to try our hearts. He fed the Israelites day by day; and he feeds us like this. We crave more than promises to live upon; and yet he never allows us to see very far in advance. It seems sometimes as if we could not get along without distrusting him. If we had but ourselves to support, we think it might be different; but we must care for our families. Perhaps a man is required, by those in whose employment he is engaged, to labour upon the Sabbath day; and the alternative seems to be, "do this, or suffer." Here is the temptation. We are asked to offend God that we may not offend man; to give up spiritual bread that we may not lose our temporal; to die spiritually that we may live naturally. We must remember that man does not live by bread alone. And it is impossible—still more, when we carefully consider the case, it is quite undesirable—that we should be free from these perplexities. Every condition of life is subject to them; if not in one form, yet in another; and all our thoughts are vain which lead us to hope that by changing our circumstances we can be free from these harassing cares. They are inseparable from the lessons of life; and to meet them wisely is the best use of life. As a scholar in passing from one class to another changes his lessons with the continual necessity for thoughtful study; as the Israelites all the way through the desert met with new trials; so we must meet these difficulties of life. Nor can we be unfeeling under them. And the discipline we must thus undergo, may be as perfect in minor as in greater things; in an humble as in an exalted sphere. Many a thorough scholar has gone forth from a log school-house, having learned his lessons from a well-thumbed spelling-book, or a second-hand arithmetic; and many a dunce has heard the lectures of learned professors in the dignified halls of a university. We must not judge of an education merely by its appliances; however much we prize the training of careful and competent teachers. And for ourselves nothing is more important than that we should carefully study what are the lessons our Great Teacher wishes us to learn. God taught the Israelites the better by putting them into straits; by showing them their weakness; by calling forth their prayers; and by displaying his grace to help. And our experience is, that many a trouble has threatened us that never hurt us;

that we have passed through many a difficulty easier than we hoped; and that the imaginary fears of the future have been more vexatious than the griefs we have realized. Let us look upon these things as TRIALS, for so they are; and let us covet the blessedness of the man who is able to endure temptation.

We should look upon these trials of life much as we look upon the training of our children. We cannot help our anxieties for them so long as we are with them. Yet we must not let these anxieties deprive them of the substantial benefits of that discipline which can only be secured by contact with the very things we dread. We are often prompted to spare them all possible exposures to fatigue and danger and temptation; we are disposed to amass for them such a property as will put them beyond the fear of want, or at least lift from them the burden of anxious exertion; we multiply our own cares by trying to carry all that they should bear. And yet wisdom tells us, that their energies of mind and body should be developed; and this can only be, by due exercise in those very matters, from which we too carefully hold them back. And experience tells us that the most useful and successful men have acquired their own property, all the better because none had been laid up for them by their parents; and that accumulated treasures laid up for our children are like the manna of the desert, which some of the disobedient Israelites would keep for to-morrow's use; and which to-morrow "bred worms and stank." It is a wise training of our children and a wise discipline of ourselves, that uses all the events of life as the Israelites used the manna. They lived upon it, day by day. And as each mouthful of the manna, insignificant in itself, yet formed part of the nourishment for the body's strength, so each event of life is in God's providence designed to call forth the actings of the spiritual life. It is impossible for us to eat bread to-day that will save us from needing bread again next week, or even to-morrow; it is not possible to lay up your strength for the body of any other person. Nor are these things desirable. Each man must live his own life, and day by day; and the profitable use of to-day is the fitting preparative for a happy to-morrow.

Moreover we are taught that the same methods of providence, the same calling forth of our own faculties, may be expected in all matters of life. There is no period of life to which we can look forward; there are no duties to which we can be called, where we may expect Divine aid, except as we are willing also to use the wisdom and the opportunities providentially afforded. If there is any case where we would expect direct Divine teachings, without regard to the promptings of human wisdom or human experience, surely it would be in providing rules for the government of God's people. The father-in-law of Moses paid him a visit in the encampment of Israel, having heard of the great things done for them against Egypt. After affectionate salutations, Moses told him, more at large, the wonders of their deliverance; and Jethro rejoiced with him, and joined him in sacrifices to the Lord. But the next day, perceiving the laborious methods by which Moses administered justice to the congregation, he found fault with him for hearing alike the most trivial and the most important cases. He suggested therefore that a different arrangement should be adopted:—That the people should be divided into classes, superior and inferior, with judges over each; and that references of only the more important and difficult cases should be made to the superior tribunals. The wisdom of this counsel is apparent; it is substantially the same as that which now prevails among ourselves, both in the state and in the church.

But the peculiar interest of this wise counsel lies in the fact that although Moses was an inspired prophet, and though we may assign to him the superior place among the men of his age, yet he adopted an imperfect and unwise system of judgment; and that a much better one was suggested by a man who in form at least, did not belong to the congregation of the Lord. And we may justly regard the whole matter as securing the Divine approval. We are not expressly told this; but the very silence of the narrative shows it. For though God rebuked the people for errors in less serious matters, there is no reproof for the adoption of this advice. We are thus taught to prize human wisdom and experience in the government of the house of God. That there are dangers from using human expedients—especially when human pride or passion suggests them—we may readily grant; but when we see Moses hearkening to the wisdom of Jethro; and when we find the Apostles of Christ discussing the great question relative to the terms upon which the Gentiles should find admission to the church; and when we recognize that both he and they were influenced by the Spirit of God, though thus wisely using the teachings of human experience, we may believe that even the influences of inspiration were not designed to supersede the intelligent use of our own faculties; that God has ever granted freedom to his people in the external ordering of his house; and that our due dependence upon Divine guidance and our earnest prayers for the influences of God's Holy Spirit upon our studies and deliberations and conclusions, are entirely consistent with the use of all advice and argument and experience to learn the truth. God never deals with us as if we were slaves, who must be directed to every duty; but as sons and freemen, who are to be taught and disciplined; and he is most honoured when a cheerful and intelligent people learn and do his will. And the line of distinction is broad between human institutions in Divine worship that contravene the principles of Scriptural teachings, and those appointments for which no direct Divine warrant is claimed, which are in full keeping with the simplicity of the gospel and which fall under the Apostle's general rule, "Let all things be done decently and in order."

CHAPTER XXV.

THE SMITTEN ROCK.

"They thirst; and waters from the rock
In rich abundance flow."

We need not carefully note the route of the Israelites through the desert, or repeat the names of their stopping-places. A record of these is made for us in the book of Numbers, ch. xxxiii. We may learn this lesson evidently, that to meet with unexpected difficulties is no proof that we are not in the path of duty. Who ever met with more trials than the people whom God himself guided?

It was not long after they left Elim and its palm trees, that the people again suffered for the want of water. Nor need we either marvel at them or censure harshly their murmurings against Moses, since alas! we may find in their rebellions too fitting a type of our own disposition to forget former mercies, when we feel the pressure of new distresses. Their exasperation was so great that Moses even stood in peril of his life. The Divine forbearance is shown towards the complaining multitude; and Moses was directed to take with him the elders of the people, and to strike a certain rock with his wonder-working rod; and water should come forth for the supply of the camp. Moses did so; and a full supply of water was immediately secured.

Several things are worthy of our attention in reference to this rock, and the water thus issuing from it.

(1.) We may notice what travellers say concerning the rock as it is found at the present day.

The traveller through these regions is shown a very remarkable rock, at some distance from Rephidim, where the Israelites were encamped, but so situated that a strong stream of water would flow down the ravines to the camp; and this rock, it is claimed, is the one smitten by the rod of Moses. The impression produced upon different travellers is various; some regard the attempt to point out the rock as resulting from the mingled superstition and imposition that have discovered and reverenced so many sacred places without any satisfactory evidence; and some are clearly convinced that the rock bears evidence for itself, that just such a miracle was once wrought there.

Mr. Stephens says "The gashes (in the rock) are singular in their appearance—they look something like the gashes in the bark of a growing tree; except that, instead of the lips of the gash swelling and growing over, they are worn, and reduced to a polished smoothness. They are no doubt the work of men's hands, a clumsy artifice of the early monks to touch the hearts of pious pilgrims."*

Dr. Robinson does not think the holes are artificial; but he declares; "As to this rock, one is at a loss whether most to admire the credulity of the monks, or the legendary and discrepant reports of travellers. It is hardly necessary to remark, that there is not the slightest ground for assuming any connection between this narrow valley and Rephidim; but on the contrary there is every thing against it."† He thinks the singularity of the rock led the monks to select it as the supposed scene of the miracle.

Other travellers however give entirely a different view of the matter. Let it suffice to quote the opinions of two other American travellers. Dr. Olin says, "The colour and whole appearance of the rock are such that, if seen elsewhere and disconnected from all traditions, no one would hesitate to believe that they (the holes in the rock) had been produced by water flowing from these fissures. I think it would be extremely difficult to form these fissures or produce these appearances by art. It is not less difficult to believe that a natural fountain should flow at the height of a dozen feet out of the face of an isolated rock. Believing, as I do, that the water was brought out of a rock belonging to this mountain, I can see

* Incidents of Travel, i. † Bib. Res. i. 166.

nothing incredible in the opinion that this is the identical rock, and that these fissures and the other appearances should be regarded as evidences of the fact."*

Dr. Durbin came there with his mind made up that the whole story touching this rock, as the one smitten by the lawgiver, was a monkish fable. But when he actually saw the rock, all his doubts vanished. He confesses that more impression was made upon him by that stone, than by any other natural object claiming to attest a miracle. He affirms that any geologist, coming across such a rock as that, ignorant of the miracle of Moses, and aware that its situation was not favourable to such a conclusion, would still decide, "that strong and long-continued fountains of water had once poured their gurgling currents from it and over it. He would not waver in his belief for a moment, so natural and so perfect are the indications. I examined it thoroughly, and if it be a forgery, I am satisfied, for my own part, that a greater than Michael Angelo designed and executed it. I cannot differ from Shaw's opinion that 'neither art nor chance, could by any means be concerned in the contrivance of these holes, which formed so many fountains.' The more I gazed upon the irregular, mouth-like chasms in the rock, the more I found my skepticism shaken; and at last I could not help asking myself, whether it was not a very

* Travels in the East, i. 417.

natural solution of the matter, that this was indeed the rock which Moses struck, that from it the waters gushed forth, and poured their streams down (the valleys) . . . . . to Rephidim, where Israel was encamped perishing with thirst."*

It is not a matter of much importance to determine the place where this wonder was wrought; yet we naturally take an interest in inquiries of this nature. We should neither be too superstitious nor too incredulous respecting scenes of such interest. It would appear that in this neighbourhood near the foot of Sinai the Israelites were encamped for about a year; and during this period they were supplied with water from this rock, which flowed forth in a steady stream passing down towards the Red Sea.

(2.) But we may next notice the supply thus furnished to the people. We have said that they remained at Horeb nearly a year. (See Numb. x. 12.) They may easily therefore during that time have received their supplies of water from the stream that issued from this rock. But it is remarkable that only upon a few occasions is there any mention made of their needing water after this. We are not indeed bound to suppose that every miracle wrought by Moses is recorded; the brevity of the narrative may exclude many. Compare John xxi. 25. Twice after this, we read of water being given to the people; once at Meribah

* Observations on the East, i. 149.

from the rock amidst the murmurings of the people, at which time Moses offended God; and again wells were dug by the lawgiver's direction. See Numb. xx., xxi. But both of these instances occurred many years after this. It may be that they often dug wells in the desert, of which no record is made. There is no natural supply of sufficient water for so large a multitude anywhere in that sterile region,* "unless water was anciently far more abundant in these regions than at present."

But the Jewish rabbis, and even some Christian commentators, including Tertullian, and among moderns Archbishop Usher, have thought that this rock followed the Israelites all through the desert,† and furnished them with water almost all the way. And this seems to be the meaning of Dr. Watts in his version of Ps. cv., where he speaks of this rock,

> "That following still the course they took
> Ran all the desert through."

Some suppose that the rock, others that the stream flowing from it, followed them through all the desert. The chief argument relied upon to prove this, is drawn from the words of Paul, "They drank of that spiritual rock that followed them." 1 Cor. x. 4.

We have no reason to judge that either the rock,

* Bib. Res., i. 106. † Shuckford's Con., iii 38.

or the water from the rock, followed the people during the journeyings of the next thirty-seven years. But it seems quite likely that a large stream of water came forth from the rock as smitten by Moses. So we find him mingling the dust of the golden calf with the water of the brook that flowed down from the mount. Deut. ix. 21. Perhaps this brook flowed off through the desert into the Red Sea by such a course that the people might often cross it during the wanderings of the next thirty-seven years; and it was not until they entirely left the southern part of their meandering route, passing from Ezion-Geber northward, that they began again to complain that they wanted water. In this sense the brook may have accompanied their march; that they crossed it sufficiently often to secure from it the water they needed.

(3.) But let us not overlook the teachings of the Apostle that this rock had a spiritual significancy, and typified Christ. He does not mean that the rock was anything more than a rock; or the water than water. He expressly says that God was displeased with many who drank of that water: his very object is to show that external advantages may be enjoyed without spiritual profit. But as the manna that nourished their bodies was also a type of that living food which God gives us for the life of the soul; so the stream from the smitten rock signified the plenteous and reviving grace of Christ. "The rock was Christ," says

Augustine, "not as to substance, but as to signification." "Christ," says Luther, "was signified by the corporeal rock of Moses."*

And these points of likeness between Christ and the rock smitten in Horeb have been suggested by an old Latin writer.

(1.) As water seems unlikely to flow from a rock, so Christ crucified, the offence of the Jews and the foolishness of the Gentiles, is the power of God unto salvation.

(2.) As waters flowed from the rock, so grace—the gifts of the Spirit so often spoken of as water—is from Christ.

(3.) As the rock gave forth no water until smitten, so only by a crucified Christ is our salvation secured.

(4.) The rock was smitten by the rod of Moses, for he was the minister of the law, under whose curse Christ suffered.

(5.) A great abundance of water flowed forth from the smitten rock; as fulness of grace is in Christ.

(6.) How vivid the comparison between a supply of water to the travellers in that desert, and salvation to the thirsty pilgrims in this wilderness-world.

(7.) As the rock supplied them long; so Christ's grace never fails.

"But in this comparison," says the same writer,

* Turrettine De Petra Christo, iv. 362.

"manifold distinctions should also be made. The rock of Moses was inanimate; Christ is the living and life-giving Rock. That had no waters in its bosom; Christ is the fountain of life and of his fulness have all we received, and grace for grace. John i. 16. That, for a time, not permanently, allayed bodily thirst; but Christ so gives us to drink his living water that we thirst no more. John iv. 14. That could not follow the Israelites; but Christ ever attends his people. Redeemed from spiritual Egypt; brought through the Red Sea of his own blood; and led by the lamp of his word through the desert of this world, he nourishes them with celestial manna, and refreshes them with living water, until they come to the celestial Canaan. There they shall hunger no more, and thirst no more, neither shall the heat nor sun smite them; for the Lamb who is in the midst of the throne shall lead them—not to streams—but to living and perennial fountains of waters, and God shall wipe away all tears from their eyes." Rev. vii. 16.*

No figure of the Scriptures is more frequently applied to Christ than that of a rock. And we have often sung in humble devotion,

"Rock of Ages cleft for me,
Let me hide myself in thee."

But if he is "the shadow of a great rock in a

* Turrettine, iv. 367.

weary land," there is even more significancy in the type of that rock in Horeb that poured out its waters to refresh that thirsting people.

What a scene for a painter's pencil* would be Moses smiting the rock, and the waters flowing down to the eager multitude. Travellers in those parched lands have described the rapid rush of man and beast to taste the desired portion. Some would bathe their very faces deep in the flowing stream; some would drink and drink again, as if they never could be satisfied; some would taste for themselves and then hasten to bear a precious draught to the feeble and the sick, who were unable to draw near the flowing waters.

And Christ in the desert of this world, is sweeter far, and more refreshing far, than the flowing waters of that smitten rock. Ho, every one that thirsteth, come ye to the waters! The Spirit and the Bride say, Come; and whosoever will let him take of the water of life freely.

* Jay's Ev. Ex., June 21. This is the subject of a famous painting by Murillo.

CHAPTER XXVI.

WAR WITH AMALEK.

"While Moses stood with arms spread wide,
Success was found on Israel's side;
But when, through weariness, they failed,
That moment Amalek prevailed." NEWTON.

THE first warfare of the children of Israel after leaving Egypt was with the Amalekites; and the enmity thus begun lasted with various intermissions through the entire records of the Old Testament history; found its close in the Empire of Persia, during the dispersion of Israel, in the death of Haman and the great day of conflict through his plot; and has been perpetuated in the memory of the Jewish people ever since, by the feast of Purim. Some have supposed that these Amalekites were descendants of Esau. But the name of Amalek, belonging to the grandson of Esau, is no sufficient proof that any tribe descended of him; and several things seem to show that the Amalekites, mentioned so often in the sacred narrative, were not descended of Esau. If even we suppose that when Balaam calls the Amalekites "the first of the nations," Numb. xxiv. 20, he but means that they were the first nation to come forth and fight against Israel; yet when we find the Amalekites mentioned in the days of Abraham, Gen. xiv. 7: that their sympathies were not with the Edomites but with the Canaanites; that they seem a more powerful and larger tribe than we would look for in a mere branch of Esau's family; and that David refers to them as "nations that were of old the inhabitants of the land as thou goest to Shur, even unto the land of Egypt," 1 Sam. xxvii. 8, we seem authorized to conclude that the Amalekites were an older nation, and quite distinct from the sons of Esau.

Where they dwelt we do not know. When Saul went against them at the command of Samuel, they dwelt "from Havilah to Shur," that is all along the northern part of the peninsula of Arabia from Canaan to Egypt—from the isthmus of Suez to the most northern point of the Persian Gulf. Josephus says they dwelt from Pelusium of Egypt to the Red Sea. (l. vii. ch. vi. § 3.) He further says that they took great pains to excite the neighbouring tribes to an early warfare against the Israelites. We may reasonably suppose that the Amalekites were a warlike tribe dwelling in the peninsula; and fearing that the Israelites would prove formidable neighbours, they resolved to attack them. But theirs was not the bold and open defiance of a manly foe. They attacked the Israelites in the rear of the hosts; when they were faint and weary; and when they anticipated no hostilities. Deut. xxv. 18. That they should do so, so soon after the overthrow of the Egyptians, and while the Israelites marched under Divine protection, greatly increased the wickedness of their warfare; and the historian adds, that they "feared not God."

In the record of Israel's earliest battle we first read the name of Joshua, who was afterwards the illustrious leader of the people; and who thus appears the military leader from Egypt to Canaan. We have no record that Moses ever actually commanded, in any of their battles. But the chief interest that belongs to the first battle of the Israelites, arises from the manner of the conflict; and the means of its successful termination. If here the people of God waged the first contest with a foe that was to contend with them for so many generations, it was fitting that we should have here a type of the church and her foes; and a significant intimation of the strength which must secure the victory over her spiritual enemies.

Moses made the arrangements for the conflict—Joshua was to lead forth chosen men, while Moses must stand upon a hill overlooking the battle, with the rod of God in his hand. The strife seems to have been fierce; lasting all the day, and having its varying fortunes. At one time it seemed as if Israel would be beaten; and at another the Amalekites were borne back. And the true strength that secured success was upon the hill top, apart from the combatants, where Moses held up the rod of God. For "it came to pass that when Moses held up his hand, Israel prevailed; and when he let down his hand, Amalek prevailed." Ex. xvii. 11. Thus evidently showing, that the holding up of the rod was a symbol of the Divine favour assisting the Israelites; and that the victory was secured, not by their own strength, but by the power of God.

That the hands of Moses were heavy is significant of the weariness of the flesh in the best of men, for the discharge of spiritual duties. As it is hard physically for any man to keep his arm extended all day towards heaven, so even believing men, believing leaders of the hosts of God's people, find it hard to maintain the true and unflagging devotion of a spiritual mind. As therefore we are told that Aaron and Hur stood on either side of Moses, and stayed up his hands, that Amalek might be entirely defeated, we have in the whole scene most precious instruction, touching the various but harmonious duties that belong to the people of God in sustaining the conflict with their enemies.

We learn here that the victories of Zion are to be secured through the earnest efforts of her sons, crowned by the blessing of God. And we may look upon the various persons here named as representing the various things to be done to secure success. Joshua and the picked men who went forth to fierce warfare, may represent the careful and earnest zeal that attempts every duty. It is not the design nor the just working of faith to lead us to neglect any of the duties God lays upon us. Truly pious labours ever depend upon the Divine blessing. So Moses stood above the fighting armies with the rod of God in his hand. But it is quite as hard to pray as it is to fight. Many a man is willing to labour hard in the cause of Zion, who yet finds it difficult to maintain a spiritual tone of feeling. Many a minister of the gospel prepares carefully for the pulpit; proclaims truthfully the doctrines of the gospel; and instructs the people with deep interest himself, and securing their attention, who yet finds it a much harder thing to enter into his closet, and hold his hands steadily up to heaven, that the hosts of the enemy may be routed. What mean the frequent appeals of even a Paul for the prayers of his brethren, except as they are a confession that his hands are heavy and that they must stay them up?

And so we are told that Aaron and Hur stayed up the hands of Moses until Amalek was defeated. They are examples of those who may stay up the hands that would otherwise droop, of them that plead with God for Israel. We do not know who Hur was. Josephus says he was the husband of Miriam. When Moses was absent in the mount, he spoke of Hur as one capable of holding, with

Aaron, rule over the camp. Ex. xxiv. 14. Thus he seems to have enjoyed the confidence of Moses. Yet very little mention is made of him; except that he was a son of Caleb; but not of that Caleb who was sent forth with the spies. In short we cannot determine who Hur was. Nor does it much matter. For they who most successfully and patiently hold up the hands of God's pleading servants may be wholly unknown, save to the ear and eye of God. Some afflicted Christian, whose feet may not even visit the sanctuary; some aged mother laid so aside by infirmities that she seems able to do little else but pray; some young and timid disciple, whose weak grasp seems incapable of clasping as yet the battle-axe for the field of stern exertion; any one among the people of God who knows that the Lord's grace, through the pleading prophet on the hill-top, is better than the heaviest strokes of the striving Joshua in the vale, may hold up the declining hands until the victory is won.

We must both strive and pray; and we often are more ready to faint at prayer than in labour. Let God's people ever help each other in addressing his throne. Let his people especially, for their own sake and for the cause's sake, hear the request of the ministry, whose place it is to plead for God, as they ask, "Brethren, pray for us." Oftentimes you are lookers on, while the minister is like Joshua, too busy now to pray; putting forth all his strength in resisting Amalek. But how feeble these efforts; how indeed will the enemy prevail in spite of all he can do, unless you act like Moses holding up your hands to heaven; or like Aaron and Hur staying up the heavy hands of those who do help him. In their various places and duties, all these were doing the same great work. We may not suppose that Moses prayed for want of courage to fight; or that Joshua fought for want of devotion to pray. The same spirit of piety actuated both; and they were fellow-helpers in the same engagements. So whether in the pulpit we labour, while in the pew you pray; or in the world you toil while in the study we pray, the same spirit belongs to the teacher and the taught. And never are our efforts more successful in resisting the world, or in winning souls, than when our hands are steadily held up towards heaven; and as they are prone to be heavy, are stayed there by our brethren's care.

CHAPTER XXVII.

MOUNT SINAI.

According to the chronology usually received, the Israelites went forth from Egypt in the year B. C. 1491. If we may receive here the Jewish tradition, it was on the fiftieth day after the Passover that they received the law from the summit of Sinai.* If this be so, the giving of the law to that people, and the outpouring of the Holy Spirit upon the disciples of Christ occurred upon the day of Pentecost.

The people were encamped at the foot of Mount Sinai; a fitting place for so grand a scene. Because the entire people were to hear the words of the Ten Commandments spoken by the voice of God, it was suitable that large grounds for their encampment should be chosen. And modern travellers tell us that there is a noble spot for an encampment, directly before the mountain. Dr. Robinson describes it, as "a fine broad plain enclosed by rugged and venerable mountains of dark

* Neither Philo nor Josephus speak of this; but later Jews affirm it; and Augustine expressly declares it. Contra Faustum Manichæum, xxxii. 1.

granite, stern, naked, splintered peaks, and ridges of indescribable grandeur; and terminated at the distance of more than a mile by the bold and awful front of Horeb, rising perpendicularly in frowning majesty from twelve to fifteen hundred feet in height. It was a scene of solemn grandeur, wholly unexpected, and such as we had never seen; and the associations which at the moment rushed upon our minds, were almost overwhelming."* Another American traveller of considerable celebrity, and still more graphic powers of description, speaks of the road to Sinai, as lying between rocky ramparts of mountains, sometimes rising to a thousand feet amidst scenes of wild sublimity. At the end of a wild defile "we came suddenly upon a plain table of ground, and before us towered in awful grandeur, so huge and dark that it seemed close to us, and barring all further progress, the end of my pilgrimage, the holy mountain of Sinai. Among all the stupendous works of nature, not a place can be selected more fitting for the exhibition of Almighty power. I have stood upon the summit of the giant Etna and looked, over the clouds floating beneath it, upon the bold scenery of Sicily and the distant mountains of Calabria; upon the top of Vesuvius and looked down upon the waves of lava, and the ruined and half-recovered cities at its foot, but they are nothing, compared with the terrific solitudes and bleak majesty of Sinai."†

* Bib. Researches, i. 130. † Stephens' Incidents of Travel.

Dr. Robinson and his companion, the Rev. Eli Smith, long a missionary in Syria and well versed in the Arabic language, did not believe that the monks at Horeb pointed out the true place of delivering the law; and they accordingly made an attempt to discover it for themselves. With much difficulty and even danger, they climbed to another peak called Es-Sŭfsâfeh; and were convinced that there the law had been delivered. Before them "lay the plain where the whole congregation might be assembled; here was the mount that could be approached and touched, if not forbidden; and here the mountain brow where the lightnings and the thick cloud would be visible, and the thunders and the voice of the trumpet be heard. . . . . . . We gave ourselves up to the impressions of the awful scene; and read, with a feeling that will never be forgotten, the sublime account of the transaction and the commandments there promulgated, in the original words as recorded by the great Hebrew legislator."*

So Dr. Durbin, another American traveller, speaks of the same peak—"One glance was enough. We were satisfied that here and here only, could the wondrous displays of Sinai have been visible to the assembled host of Israel; that here the Lord spoke with Moses; that here was the mount that trembled and smoked in the presence of its Creator. We gazed for some time in silence and

* Biblical Researches, i. 158.

when we spoke, it was with a reverence that even the most thoughtless of our company could not shake off."

And yet these observing travellers are not certainly correct. For at the base of the mountain usually taken for the spot for the delivery of the law, and upon a side which they did not observe, there is a large plain as suitable for the encampment of Israel; but which cannot be seen from the path usually taken by travellers, and has therefore been overlooked.

But in either view of the case, no place in the world has more solemn and awful associations than those that gather around Sinai. What a declaration was that when God announced to the people that he would come down in their sight; and as they were surrounded by these scenes of awful sublimity in the silence of the desert, and gazed upon the rising precipices that seemed to penetrate the sky and lose themselves in the clouds, how impressive the thought of the Divine presence in such a place as that.

They were required to sanctify themselves against the third day, and to gather around the foot of this magnificent mountain. Yet they were forbidden to touch it. And on the third day, God came down in terrible majesty. Even Moses, the favoured one, "exceedingly" feared and trembled, Heb. xii. 21; and all the people were afraid. There were thunderings and lightnings and the peal of the trumpet sounding above the thunder; and Mount Sinai was full of smoke; and then the voice of the Most High himself proclaimed in their ears from that trembling summit all the words of the ten commandments. After this he gave this law to Moses, engraven by his own finger upon two tables of stone. These two tables were broken by Moses in holy indignation at the sin of the people; and as a solemn token that they had broken the law and the covenant of God. But God was pleased to renew these tables by the hand of Moses; and by his own hand, a second time, to write the law upon them. This second pair of tables was preserved by the Israelites with religious care in the Ark of the Covenant for more than nine hundred years; (from B. C. 1491 to 588), and they were finally lost in the burning of Solomon's temple.

We are told in several places of the Scriptures that this great law was given upon Sinai by the ministry of angels. We do not understand by this, that Jehovah was not present; on the contrary his powerful presence is expressly asserted. God himself spoke and wrote that law. But his majesty and glory were exhibited amidst crowds of attending ministers. The New Testament writers three several times declare the presence of angels when the law was given. So the martyr Stephen declared to the Jews that they had received the law by the ministry of angels, (Acts

vii. 53); and Paul in the Epistle to the Galatians declares that it was "ordained by angels;" (Gal. iii. 19); and in the Epistle to the Hebrews (ii. 2), he calls it "the word spoken by angels." In the Old Testament, Moses declares the same thing. He says, "The Lord came from Sinai, and rose up from Seir unto them; he shined forth from Mount Paran, and he came with ten thousands of saints (or holy ones); from his right hand went forth his fiery law for them." Deut. xxxii. 2. And the Psalmist in the lxviii. Psalm declares that when the earth shook and Sinai trembled at the presence of God, there were with him twenty thousand chariots and thousands of angels. The law was given amidst the attendance and in some degree by the ministry of angels. See also Ps. xviii. for like imagery.

Before declaring this law, God called Moses up into the mount. From this interview he came down to prepare the people for the awful scenes before them. And after they heard the thunder and the trumpet, they so greatly feared that they entreated Moses to act the part of mediator between them and the Lord. It would seem then that during the declaration of the Ten Commandments themselves, Moses was among the people. Ex. xx. 19; and in their dread assured them that God but proved them to put his fear before them that they might not sin. Afterwards Moses drew near into the thick darkness where God was; and received other communications of the Divine will, respecting the government of the people, the building of the tabernacle, and the regulation of the worship of God under the Levitical economy.

www.ingramcontent.com/pod-product-compliance
Lightning Source LLC
LaVergne TN
LVHW010222110826
845151LV00004B/1173